The  et

How to
SHINE IN EXAMINATIONS
AND LIFE!

by

DENNIS B. JACKSON, B.A.

Honours Graduate in English of Manchester University.
Formerly Station Education Officer, Royal Air Force
Wilmslow

Melvin Powers
Wilshire Book Company

12015 Sherman Road, No. Hollywood, CA 91605

© A. G. ELLIOT
MCMLIV
© A. G. ELLIOT 2nd edition
MCMLX

All Rights Reserved
Printed in the United States of America

ISBN 0-8780-033-X

CONTENTS

5

Shining Rule

"It isn't a matter of knowing all about your subject it's a matter of knowing all about exams."

That is the belief upon which this book is based. I have met scores of sad students who will testify to its truth. They have failed exams. not through ignorance of their subjects, but through ignorance of examination technique.

To such students, who have failed—or fear to fail—exams. through inexperience or "examination nerves", this book should prove of great value.

It is especially dedicated to them.

FOREWORD

By G. E. Grace

A LONG-HAIRED, bespectacled, pale-faced, industrious student works for fourteen hours every day. He has read widely on his subject. He can discuss it most learnedly. Everybody knows he is the most industrious student in the school.

A second pupil—who never seems to do any work, but who spends his time playing football and cricket—mixes freely with his fellows. Nobody expects him to shine in the exams.

The examinations arrive, and after them the weeks of waiting. And then the results. What do we find?

Strangely enough, the long-haired intellectual has gained only a moderate mark, while the open scholarship has gone to his carefree rival. This happens all over the country. The superior scholar is defeated by a less studious colleague. The reason for this lies in examination technique.

It is not the best student nor the best scholar who gains the highest marks in. examinations. It is the scholar with the greatest knowledge of *examination technique.*

EXAMINATION TECHNIQUE

A lot can be said about examination technique. There are many techniques. Books have been written proclaiming many weird and wonderful processes of study, many of which are based on sound sense and experience and have saved the student time and have planned his study efficiently.

But in this book the author presents an entirely new and brilliant method. It alters the whole conception of planned study habits previously published, and it enables exceptional marks to be gained by the average pupil with only 25 per cent of the work that the average schoolmaster now forces his pupils to carry out. The author of this book and devisor of this plan has put his theory into operation, and incredible results have been achieved. He first conceived

7

this method as a scholar himself, and planned his early studies in accordance with it.

The results were as follows:

School Certificate (normally taken by the best pupils in grammar schools at the age of sixteen) *passed at the age of fourteen* with three distinctions and four credits. *Higher School Certificate* (normally taken by students—who are specially selected for Sixth-form work—at the age of eighteen) *passed at the age of sixteen* with very good in History and good in English Literature (the only two subjects taken). At the same age in University Scholarship examinations he gained excellent in Scholarship English and good in Scholarship History, and on these results he was awarded a University Scholarship to study English. He then progressed through an honours degree course and gained Bachelor of Arts (with honours) when nineteen, being the youngest graduate of the year at his University.

It is no longer possible, by the Education Act, for any scholar to repeat these feats at the same age, although some headmasters still enter examination candidates at an early age. The author of this book has systematised his study methods, and you will be able to read them in this volume. He has previously passed the system for trial to only one scholar. This boy received the details at the age of twelve when commencing his grammar school education. By using the methods described he also passed School Certificate at the age of fourteen and also gained University Scholarship at the age of sixteen. He has since progressed to Oxford University where he has made his mark as soccer captain.

This success meant that this plan of examination technique had to be published. Here it is! It will enable you to achieve higher marks in examinations than you ever dreamed of! Great results with a minimum of study!

If you are taking an examination, this book is meant for you. If your children are at school, you should ensure that they have a chance to read it.

It is the " Open Sesame " to examination success.

PART ONE

ALICE AND THE MAGICAL LESSONS

INTRODUCING ALICE

A LITTLE girl sits at home, quiet but worried. She is " doing her homework ".

Or, to be more accurate, she is " not doing her home-work ": she is looking at her homework. She is looking quite intently. She is reading again and again the only three words that she has written, neatly inscribed at the top of the page:

" My Home Town."

She reads the three words again. She bites her pen. She gazes at the ceiling for inspiration, and dazedly watches the gyrations of a house-fly. She stares once more at the three insistent words at the top of her page.

She is sad and bewildered, this little girl, for she has to write an essay.

.   .   .   .   .

Poor Alice! In front of her is a task of self-expression, a job that should have brought to her the joy of creation and the thrill of literary activity. But all it brings to her is un-certainty and annoyance.

She is worried. It is not simply that she must write an essay (which she hates), but also that when she goes to school she has to study many other things which she finds only moderately interesting, and that eventually she will have to take examinations (which she is certain she will fail).

Yes, Alice is worried.

.   .   .   .   .

What a terrible tragedy! If only someone would help her! If only someone could show her how to enjoy essay-writing and make her eager to write! If only she could learn the

9

delight of literature. If only she could glimpse, in some magical way, the beautiful land of literature and the adventure of ideas. If only she could be given a vivid bright presentation of those subjects that had always been taught so dully. If only she could be shown how to dispel her dread of examinations and replace it by a gay, vital zest for them! If only she could be given a plan that would make her see all her studies in a dazzling new light and give her the secret of " How to Shine in Examinations "!

Yes. If only Alice could have some magical lessons! If only she could see, in a beautiful vision, the royal road past all her examinations. If only she could follow a new, brilliant plan that could carry her in triumph through every test she attempted.

" If only I could have some magical lessons," thought Alice.

Many others are wishing the same wish, for there are many people in the same position. Not all of them are little girls— some are solemn-faced University students certain they are going to " pip " finals; some are National Servicemen having a try for promotion in the forces; some are insurance clerks who must pass their prelims.; some are schoolboys who never seem able to concentrate; some are sixth-formers who know their subjects backwards but always " go to pieces " in the examination room; and there are millions more.

Just like Alice, they all need a stimulating new formula for examination success. They would all like some magical lessons.

And luckily for them, Alice received some magical lessons.

And (also luckily for them) these lessons are printed in this book for all to read.

CHAPTER ONE

" OPEN SESAME " TO EXAMINATIONS!

" WELL! " said Alice, " I've been sitting here for half an hour racking my brains, but I still can't do my homework. I know how to read essays, but I want to find out how to write them. After all, before I'm Alice M.A. I've got to pass lots of exams."

" Here, did I hear you say exams.?" said a voice.

" Yes, I did," Alice replied. " Who are you?"

"I'm an expert in exams.," said the voice. " Passed them all easy as wink. Not only gained my degree, but got a first-class one. Every exam. I've ever taken I've come top."

" Have you really?" said Alice eagerly.

" I have," the voice replied. " And I've never done a lot of hard work. My secret was *essays*. I wrote marvellous essays. You see, nearly *all* exams., even science exams., include essays. Lots of exams. are nothing but essays. So if you know the secrets of essay-writing—as I do—you're well away."

" Will you tell me your secrets?" Alice asked. " You'll help me a lot."

" Don't mind if I do," said the voice. " I've passed all my examinations now, but I'd like to help *you*."

" Thank you very much, sir," Alice said.

" No need to call me, ' sir '," said the voice. " I'm an ordinary fellow, even if I have got a first-class honours degree."

" Thank you," said Alice. " Please tell me how to write essays."

" All right," the voice went on. " But I'm not going to say much about the mechanics of essay-writing, mind. I expect you know how to string two sentences together, and how to link up your paragraphs, and so on."

"I think I do," Alice replied.

" Well, if you don't," said the voice, " there's lots of books that will teach you that sort of thing far better than I can."

" Then just what will you teach me?" Alice asked.

" Something ten times as important. My examination technique, so to speak. You know, it isn't the best *scholar* that does best in exams. It's technique that does it. You see, exams. aren't really fair. Exams. are like cricket matches, only everybody's judged on one or two innings. In those innings a first-rate batsman like Peter May might only make about ten runs; some other chap, say XYZ of Lancashire, who isn't a real batsman at all, might have more luck and hit sixty. Exams. are like that. They don't measure true scholastic ability: they measure journalistic prowess, steady nerves, good luck and, above all, examination technique. Now, Alice, that's where I can help you."

" But I'm not taking any big exams. yet," said Alice.

" No," the voice replied: " but you have your difficulties, and I can suggest the way to avoid them. Essays don't figure in your examinations very prominently, but where they do come they are very important."

" In our exams.," said Alice, " there's only an English paper where there's an essay, and you only have to do *one* essay on that paper."

" You're speaking about English Language or Grammar or Composition examinations, aren't you?" the voice asked: " I mean, you don't take an English Literature paper, do you?"

" Well, we do," Alice replied, " though I was thinking of the Grammar paper."

" Quite," said the voice: " I know just what you mean. You have an examination in which you have to answer several grammar questions, about punctuation, analysis, parts of speech and so on."

" That's right," Alice assured him: " then there's also an essay question."

" Yes, I know. You have a choice of about five general subjects, such as ' Superstitions ' or ' Railway Stations '."

" Yes," said Alice: " but they're always such *difficult* subjects. I can never think what to write."

" I see. I know that a lot of boys and girls of your age have the same trouble. In fact, I must admit that even I——"

Alice thought that the voice really was conceited, but she needed help so badly. " I feel so silly speaking to a voice," she said. " Can't you let me have a look at you?"

" I could," the voice said: " but I won't. You interrupted my train of thought. What was I saying?"

" You said, sir," Alice replied, " that even you, when you were my age, had trouble with your essays."

" Oh, yes, to be sure," the voice said: " and I don't mind giving you the benefit of my experience. I remember that when I first went to the grammar school I had to write an essay on ' A Walk in the Country '. Now, being town-bred, and knowing nothing about trees or birds (as a matter of fact I still don't know a starling from a thrush, or a larch from a beech), I wrote a very bad essay."

Alice was very pleased to hear that even this wonderful fellow could make mistakes, but she knew that she had undergone similar experiences many times and that advice here would be invaluable.

" Alice, do you know why it was a poor essay?" the voice asked.

" I suppose it was because you wrote about things that you didn't understand. Still, nobody can blame you for that; the subject was one with which you were unfamiliar."

" Ah, but *I was* at fault," the voice said. " I should have written about things that I *did* know."

" I don't see how you could have done that," Alice replied. " The subject didn't suit you."

" I should have made it suit me," the voice explained.

" How do you mean?" Alice asked.

" I should have written about something that interested me. I was very keen on cricket at that time, so I should have written an essay about cricket."

" You couldn't do that," Alice objected, " because the subject wasn't ' Cricket '; it was ' A Walk in the Country '."

" Ah, but I could," said the voice. " I could have begun like this, for example:

" 'A WALK IN THE COUNTRY'

" ' One day last summer I decided to go for a walk in the countryside. I took the train to a small village and arrived at two o'clock. I set off walking down a cobbled village street. Soon I was among the lanes——'

" As a matter of fact," the voice said, " I did begin my original bad essay in that way, and then I went on to digress regarding the various flora and fauna I saw. Of course, I should have continued like this:

" ' As I walked along one lane, I saw that a cricket match was in progress. A well-built, red-faced villager was merrily hitting half-hearted off-spinners all round the wicket. A red-headed fast-bowler came on to bowl, and his second ball brought a vigorous Duckworthian appeal from a lanky wicket-keeper. The umpire said " not out ", much to the displeasure of loud-voiced local supporters . . .' "

" I'm beginning to understand," Alice said.

" Good. You see, I was at home writing about cricket, but I was very ignorant about linnets and bluebells."

" I see," Alice said. " You mean that I must write about the things that really interest me."

" Of course," the voice answered. " And once you understand that principle you'll find it easy to understand everything that I'm going to tell you."

" You've helped me quite a lot already," Alice told him.

" I'm glad you don't think the point unimportant," said the voice. " I'll show you how it affects even the most advanced examinations. That will be later, of course."

" Thank you again," Alice said. " What's your next lesson about essays?"

" My next point is a really vital one. I think that I can best explain it by asking you a question. Do you mind, or is it too much like school?"

Alice thought it was becoming rather like a school lesson, but the voice was making her school life seem much easier. " Please ask me anything you wish," she said.

" Very well," said the voice, and stated this question: " How would you start an essay on, say, ' Cats '?"

Alice thought for a minute, then decided that her essay would start off in this way:

" CATS

" Cats are four-legged, furry little animals, and they are kept as pets.

" There are also lions and tigers, however, which are also known as cats.   They live in jungles and can be seen at the Zoo——"

Alice couldn't think what to say next, so she paused, hoping that the voice would help her, but all the voice said was:

" Anything else?"

" I don't think there is," Alice faltered.

" Haven't you been listening to me?" said the voice.

" Oh, yes," said Alice eagerly.   " I know what you mean. I should write about something that I do know about.   And yet, I can't think of any interests connected with cats."

" I agree that it's not very easy," said the voice in a kindly manner; " if you were a boy and fond of adventure stories you could mention the pirate's type of ' cat '—the ' cat-o'-nine-tails ', you know.   Then you might write a sentence about those ' cats' eyes ' that we have on our roads.   I don't expect those ideas will appeal to you a great deal, but perhaps you can think of something."

" How about proverbs?" asked Alice.

" What do you mean?" said the voice.

" Well, you know," Alice replied, " proverbs like ' A cat can look at a king ' or ' Curiosity killed the cat '."

" Oh yes, Alice; that's very good!   Then you might write a little bit about cats in nursery rhymes and pantomimes."

" I know!" cried Alice: " ' Dick Whittington ' and ' Puss in Boots '.   I don't know how I'd get all these things down in an exam.!"

" There you are, you see," said the voice: " and a minute ago you couldn't think of anything.   Your mistake was in sticking so closely to the subject.   Let your thoughts wander, and you'll never be stuck.   And that applies to every exam. you'll ever take."

" Thank you," cried Alice: " now I really know how to write an essay on ' Cats '."

" Not quite," said the voice: " there's a very important point that you've missed."

" Surely not! " Alice retorted; " I could write about the domestic cat, the larger cats, the cat-o'-nine-tails, the cat in literature and lots of other things."

" I agree that you've found many facts," said the voice; " but what about your readers? Have all your facts told them anything that they didn't know?"

Alice wondered. " No, I don't think so. They're all well-known things."

" That's right," said the voice. " You began, if I remember rightly, by saying that ' a cat has four legs and that it is a furry animal kept as a pet '. Now, who's delighted to learn that? Nobody—because everyone knows it."

" I suppose it wouldn't be very interesting," said Alice. " Yet what can I do? I don't know anything about cats except those things that everybody knows."

" That's just where you're wrong," said the voice. " You must always think of the great essayist, Montaigne. He spoke to paper as to the first man that he met. And because of that he was the father of all essayists."

" Yes, but what has that got to do with my essay about ' Cats '?"

" Well, you'll understand if you answer this question. If you were walking along the road and you saw one of your friends and you decided to say something connected with cats, what would you say?"

Alice thought hard for a moment.

" What I mean is," went on the voice, " you certainly wouldn't start telling your friend that a cat had four legs and that some cats are black and some tabby."

" No, I wouldn't do that," Alice agreed.

" Then, if you said anything at all about cats, just what would you say?"

" I think I know! " Alice cried: " I suppose I'd talk about my own little pet, Kitty."

" You've got it! You see, you *do* know something about

cats that other people don't know. You'll always be interesting in your essays if you write from your own experience; speak unto paper as to the first man that you meet."

"But do people want to hear about my little doings?" Alice asked.

"You bet they do!" the voice cried: "people are interested in other people, and they are especially interested in trivialities. They don't want a lecture on the subject of cats, but they like to know about *your* cat, and *your* opinions about cats and about *you*. Never forget that!"

"That's exactly the opposite of what they've told me at school," said Alice. "They said that I should never write the word ' I '."

"That may apply to a geographical or historical essay," the voice explained, "but when you write an essay on an English Language paper, ' I ' is the best word of them all."

Alice must have still seemed puzzled, because the voice went on to add: "If you've ever read any of Charles Lamb's essays you'll know that he was always talking about himself."

"Yes," said Alice: "he was fond of running himself down."

"That's known as self-depreciation," the voice explained. "All the modern essayists write about themselves. They put forward their own opinions, or relate their own experiences."

"So they do," Alice said. "Now I come to think of it, ' Alpha of the Plough ' did that with his essay on W. G. Grace. He wrote about playing truant from school to watch him, and, as you say, his own opinions."

"That's right; he didn't give details of all W.G.'s averages and records. You see, that would have been an *account*, and ' Alpha of the Plough ' was writing an essay."

"I see," said Alice, "I'm sorry that I didn't grasp the point sooner."

"Don't worry, Alice," comforted the voice: "boys and girls much older than you often make those mistakes. In a School Certificate examination one year there was an essay to be done on ' Neighbours ', and one of the markers told me that he looked forward to reading those essays. He wanted

B

to read what the pupils thought about Mr. Next-door who wouldn't let children play in the street and Mrs. Over-the-road who was always grumbling at everyone and the Neighbour family who kept the radio blaring all night and banged about whenever there was homework to be done—you can see the possibilities, can't you?"

"Yes," Alice replied: "and did they write those things?"

"They didn't," said the voice. "Most of the essays began like your ' Cats ' effort. You know, ' Neighbours are people who live next door, though in the country neighbours may be many miles away ', etc. etc. They were nearly all bad essays, just because the candidates had failed to write from personal experience."

"This is very helpful," said Alice; "nobody's ever explained these things to me before."

"I'm glad you're interested," replied the voice. "I can see that you're going to gain a high mark in your School Certificate."

"But I'm not taking that exam. for years," Alice said.

"What a pity!" said the voice. "I could help you such a lot."

"Well," said Alice, "I've got two friends who are taking their matriculation in July, and my brother passed it last year, and so he's in the Sixth Form now. They'd be even more interested than I am."

"Capital!" cried the voice: "suppose we meet at the same time to-morrow, and you bring your friends along. I'll be pleased to help them."

"Thank you so much," said Alice: "I'm sure they'll love to come. But—er—don't you think that they might think that I was a little bit *odd* if I say that I'm being taught by a *voice*?"

"What? In these days of radio and television? Surely not! And if you all listen carefully to-morrow," the voice continued, "I might even materialise! Good-bye!"

CHAPTER TWO

PASSING SCHOOL-LEAVING EXAMINATIONS

"Come on, Alice," said Barbara: "where's your illustrious 'voice'?"

"He should be here by now," Alice replied. "We must all sit down and keep quiet."

They all sat down and kept quiet for what seemed like five minutes, then Alice's brother, Roger, said: "I hope you're not teasing us, Alice. I could be reading my 'Virgil', instead of sitting here."

"You want some help with your exams., don't you?" Alice retorted, rather snappily. ("Roger is so tiresome at times," she thought.)

"I *do* hope the voice comes," said Angela, who was always excited over everything.

"Be quiet, all of you!" snapped Alice, who felt very proud of being able to order them about. ("They may be older than me," thought Alice to herself; "but it's *my* 'ghost'".)

"Oh, I can hear something!" cried Angela.

"Hush!" exclaimed the others, and Roger said:

"It's only a motor-car in the road."

"How do we address him when he does arrive?" asked Barbara: "we can't just call him 'Voice'!"

"Then call me 'Genius'!" said someone. The voice had arrived.

"He really *is* conceited," Alice thought to herself: "I'm certainly not going to call him 'Genius'!" Then, aloud, she added: "Hullo! I've brought Barbara and Angela, and this is Roger."

"Pleased to meet you all," said the voice.

Angela was half frightened and half thrilled by this voice that came from nowhere. "Are you going to help us pass our examination?" she asked.

" Certainly," replied the voice: " I know all about the General Certificate of Education at Ordinary Level, and naturally everything that I say applies to equivalent examinations."

" That will suit me!" exclaimed Angela; " but Roger has passed his G.C.E. He probably wants something of a more advanced nature."

" I can provide it," said the voice: " that will be later; but I think my remarks for the rest of you will interest Roger too."

" It's lovely to listen to the voice of an expert!" said Angela.

" Thank you," replied the voice of the Expert. " Now, the Ordinary Level G.C.E. is a most important examination, and it has been made to appear so vital in life. And there will always be examinations and tests of all sorts and sizes—and, as for poor Roger, there are never any signs of the abolition of the higher exams."

" I rather like exams.," said Roger, but the girls all looked at him so fiercely that he didn't dare say any more.

" The Ordinary Level," began the voice of the Expert, " demands a fair knowledge of many subjects. You should be a Jack-of-all-studies, and it doesn't matter if you're master of none. My theory states that ability to write good essays will ensure success. Essays are so very important in English Literature and History, while in English Language most of the marks are allotted for two big questions, (1) Comprehension; (2) Essay. The comprehension demands no skill, and normal intelligence will bring you a pass, so the real test is the essay, and I'll give you some hints in a moment. So in Ordinary G.C.E. you'll find that essays are all-important on the ' arts ' side. Even in the ' scientific ' subjects the same principle applies. Geography demands good essays——"

" But not literary essays," Roger broke in. " You mean précis-like accounts."

" Quite," agreed the Expert: " you must say what you mean tersely and well. Your aim should be *multum in parvo*. In fact, you must be able to *write*: you must be an essayist."

" What about Science itself?" asked Barbara. " Surely essays don't matter in that paper?"

"They certainly do," replied the Expert. "General Science demands a superficial knowledge of a truly enormous variety of subjects, all of which are linked in some way with science. Science is such a wide term, however, that the General Science paper comes to be similar to an advanced General Knowledge examination. There are a lot of scientific facts to learn, but once again general knowledge and good essays will see you through."

"If we pass those five subjects that you've mentioned," said Barbara, "we've gained a good certificate."

"It sounds simple," Angela said; "but many people fail: there is a lot to learn!"

"There is indeed. But those scholars who fail their Certificate usually miss the boat not because they don't know their facts, but *because they lack examination experience.* You see, for most pupils it is the first big public exam."

"Yes," said Barbara: "that's why everyone feels so nervous about it. It's because they have no examination experience."

"And therefore no examination technique," endorsed the Expert.

"And will you tell us how it's done?" asked Angela, excited as ever.

"Certainly," said the Expert: "I've already shown you that essays are the key to the whole issue."

"And you gave *me* " (it was Alice speaking) " some hints on essay-writing."

"And now you wish to know how to use your knowledge in the examination room?"

"That's it!"

"Well," said the voice: "which exam. should I talk about?"

"Ordinary G.C.E. for me!" cried Angela.

"Yes, but which paper? How about English Language?— the essay is most important in that paper."

"All right," said Barbara, "English Language. But you must help us with other subjects afterwards."

"Very well," agreed the Expert. "I think you know the general shape of English Language papers. They're all very similar, whether Ordinary level or Advanced (where it's only a subsidiary paper, I think). You are set a hefty comprehension question, followed by an essay, followed by various grammar exercises, usually making five questions in all. O.K.?"

The others nodded.

The Expert continued: " I can't stress too strongly the importance of those first two questions. Examiners want to know (a) that you can understand English; (b) that you can write it. Grammar isn't quite so essential. Those grammar questions matter, but the comprehension and essay eclipse them. The most difficult point about answering grammar questions is the time factor: you never know *how long* it is going to take you."

" Hear, hear," said Roger. " When I took my English paper I mastered the comprehension fairly quickly, then I spent the amount of time on which I had decided writing the essay——"

" I can guess the rest!" the Expert said. " You were through the grammar section in no time."

" Yes, and I was left with lots of time on my hands."

Barbara seemed a little puzzled. " Surely it's a good thing to finish quickly. And, after all, you could have added more to your essay in the time that was left," she said.

Roger frowned a little. " Not so easy," he said. " I had worked out the essay according to plan; each paragraph dovetailed into the scheme of things; the ending was smooth and melodious. If I had started to add a point here and alter a line there, I would have spoilt the whole piece."

The Expert agreed that Roger was wise not to meddle with a well-constructed essay.

" But what about the wasted time?" Angela asked.

" I'm coming to that," the Expert said. " It's suicidal to sit in an exam. room if you're not writing hard."

" You've got to think as well as write," Barbara exclaimed.

" Not at all," said the Expert. " In subjects such as mathematics or Latin you must spend a lot of time in *thinking*, but in most other papers time spent in that way is time wasted. I'll explain later on. Just for the moment let me advise you on this question of the English Language paper. It's very important, because it will crop up in nearly every exam. you'll ever take. Now let me ask you for *your* views. How would *you* tackle the paper Roger misjudged? You remember what he told us. He finished the compulsory comprehension question and then the essay question in the time he had allotted himself. The rest of the paper was very easy to him; he quickly finished it, and then found that he had to spend the last half-hour twiddling his thumbs and reading through his efforts. Now, how would *you* approach such a paper?"

Everyone was shy of speaking, as school-children usually are. Angela was usually good at breaking awkward silences, so Alice looked very hard at her until she said: " Well, I suppose Roger should have studied more past papers, then he would not have left so much time for his grammar questions which he finished so quickly."

" I beg your pardon!" exclaimed Roger, a little angrily. Then, taking advantage of his slender seniority, he added: " My dear little child, I knew all there was to know about the paper. The grammar *might* have been very difficult——"

" But you could have looked to see the grammar section *before* starting your answer paper, and judged how much time the grammar would take. Then you could have arranged the time accordingly." Angela had said this very boldly, and Roger seemed stumped for a reply, so she went on enthusiastically: " I mean, if you saw the grammar was easy, you could have given yourself longer for the essay. If the grammar looked hard, you would shorten the essay."

Roger still didn't know what to say, but the voice of the Expert gave his verdict.

" You know, Roger, she's got something there. You mustn't stick too strictly to a plan of campaign decided *outside* the examination room *before* you've seen the paper!"

" No, I suppose not," said Roger. " It's like deciding that you'll cut the next ball when you bat at cricket. You should really play each ball on its merits."

" Yes," said the Expert. " Roger is quite right. As Roger says, the time spent in deciding which questions to attempt is really time lost. Now, I want you all to think again, and let's see if we can find a better solution than Angela's.''

They all thought again.

After some moments Barbara said: '' I suppose Roger should have written the essay all but the ending, then left a blank space, and continued with grammar.''

'' This sounds a good idea!'' the Expert cried. '' Barbara says that Roger should have apportioned a certain number of minutes (say, forty) for his essay. After that he should have written the opening of his essay and also many paragraphs, until the forty minutes had passed. He would then leave a blank page or so. Now, if the grammar questions were ones that could be answered at sight, Roger would rush through them, then return to his essay, add as many further points as time allowed, and then, finally, he would close with an ending paragraph. Well, what do you think of that idea, Roger?''

'' It's better than making my mistake, of course,'' Roger said. '' Actually, though, the thing isn't fool-proof. When I took my examination, it was stated that no space must be left between answers. Besides, even if you can leave a space, there are still difficulties. But it was a very good suggestion, just as Angela's was.''

'' But not quite right, eh?'' asked the Expert. '' Well, come on all of you! Any more bright ideas?''

Silence.

'' You've been very warm,'' said the Expert.

Everyone still looked puzzled.

'' *You* tell us, please,'' Alice said to the Expert.

'' Well, here's a hint,'' the voice replied. '' In what *order* would you answer the questions?''

'' Oh, of course!'' cried Angela. '' You'd leave the essay to the end.''

'' That's it,'' agreed Barbara. '' You'd answer the comprehension and the grammar—then you'd spend the rest of the time on the essay.''

'' Well done!'' congratulated the Expert.

But Roger wasn't satisfied.

'' I'm not sure about that,'' he said. '' You told us that

the essay was most vital. If it's left to the end of the paper you won't be fresh; you'll tend to be careless.''

'' That's a good point,'' the Expert said.

'' And in addition,'' Roger went on, '' you may find yourself without enough time for the essay. Since it is the most important item on the paper, it mustn't be hurried.''

'' Another good point,'' said the Expert, '' but I think you are mistaken.''

'' Why?'' asked Roger.

'' First, because I maintain that you won't be too tired to write a good essay at the end of the paper. You see, English Language is a short, unacademic exam. that you should enjoy. There should be no question of losing freshness.''

'' Yes, perhaps so,'' Roger said. '' What about my other point? You might have to rush your essay.''

'' There's no harm in spending only a little time on your essay. If you find that you have only twenty minutes left for the essay instead of thirty or forty, you can easily write a short essay. Quantity is not as important as quality.''

'' I think I agree now,'' said Roger. '' It's easier to adapt an essay to the time allowed than to fit in a grammar question.''

'' Yes, and if you have time to spare you can continue writing your essay until the last moment. There's no time wasted, and the paper is certain to be finished.''

'' It's a good plan,'' said Roger. '' If you complete half a grammar question because of the time factor you can only score half marks.''

'' Exactly. Yet a half-length essay can bring you near to full marks.''

'' Good,'' said Roger. '' Then the moral is ' Leave the essay to the end '.''

Barbara and Angela and Alice seemed convinced that this was the best plan, and Barbara was quick to ask the Expert to tell them how to write essays at School Certificate standard.

'' Much depends upon individual ability,'' the Expert replied. '' I've already mentioned some pointers to Alice. Perhaps she'll pass them on.''

Alice nodded. '' You told me to write in the same way as

I spoke. You suggested that I should be perfectly natural. I should be personal and chatty, and stretch the subject so that I could hold forth on things that interested me."

" Very good," said the Expert. " If you bear those points in mind, then you won't go wrong. Now you would like me to indicate the standard required."

" Please! " exclaimed Angela.

" Well, you will naturally reach a higher standard in home-work essays than in the exam. itself. Let's have a look at an essay I wrote in my School Certificate year."

When the Expert had finished reading, Angela cried (rather cheekily, Alice thought), " Not so dusty, old boy! "

" If your homework essays are of that length and standard you needn't worry about English Language," said the Expert.

Really, he is a little conceited, Alice told herself; fancy using his own work as a standard. Besides, she had heard some of that essay somewhere before.

The Expert continued to boast so much of his essay that Alice was boiling inwardly. At last she could scarcely contain herself. " He's asked for it," she thought, and she declared aloud: " You really needn't give yourself airs about that essay. I've been reading all ' Alpha of the Plough's ' books and half of your essay is stolen from him."

" So you've found me out, eh, Alice? " smiled the Expert. " I'll have to tell you a little story."

Alice hardly knew what to expect, but the Expert seemed a little upset, so she didn't interrupt him any further.

" Once upon a time," laughed the Expert, " I was watching an England cricketer—a very famous one—at net practice. The first ball I watched was driven by this batsman tremendously. ' However did you learn to crack a ball like that?' I asked him. ' There's a knack in it,' he replied. ' Frank Wesley taught me how to do it.' The next ball was a short, slow one, and the batsman skipped out to drive it on the half-volley. Then he turned round: ' Another England player showed me that one—Eddie Paynter.' The next ball was hit with lovely charm. ' Cyril Washbrook coached me for hours over that shot.' And so on, and so on."

" I see what you mean," said Alice.

" Good! " the Expert replied. " There is nothing wrong in using a phrase similar to that of another writer here and there——"

" But you said ' Be yourself '," objected Barbara.

" Yes, yes. By all means write in an individual style. But build up your own style by gathering the honey from the flowers of literature." The Expert seemed to think his metaphor very clever, for he paused, as though awaiting applause. As a second thought, he continued: " One does not need to worry too much about copyright laws *in an exam.*"

" But what's all this got to do with exams.?" Angela cried, impatient as ever.

" I'm glad you asked that," said the Expert. " I want to tell you how I used to prepare for my English Language exams."

" That's what we want to hear," said Alice.

" I've already stressed the importance of the essay question," the Expert began; " the other questions are——"

" Plain common-sense?" Roger suggested.

" Exactly. And they require an alert mind. So it isn't advisable to clutter up your brain with swotting."

" I see," said Roger. " So spend the night before your English exam. at the pictures."

" Not quite," laughed the Expert: " yet, nevertheless, spend it enjoyably. The essay is important, so it's a good idea to spend an hour on the eve of the exam. reading through a good book of popular modern essays."

" Your friend A. G. Gardiner again, I suppose," smiled Barbara.

" Yes. And there are plenty of other essayists too. I have a strong affection for ' Alpha of the Plough ' because I used him as a guide to essay-writing in my schooldays. Detective-Inspector Alice has just exposed me!"

They all smiled, but Angela didn't quite understand the issue, and she was determined to fathom it.

" Please," she said to the Expert: " when you said that you spent the evening before the exam. ' reading popular modern essays ', did you mean that you simply skipped through them for pleasure or that you studied them?"

" Oh, I certainly didn't mean learn them by heart as a task. Just read for interest. If by any chance you read the same essayist a great deal, you will possibly know a number of phrases that have endeared themselves to your memory. That is how I felt about ' Alpha of the Plough '."

" But there's no need to learn lines——"

" Goodness me, no! Just read ten or a dozen little essays —more if you wish—and you should remember the main themes when the next day dawns with its examinations."

" And is that all we need to do?" asked Alice.

" Yes, except for the rather obvious procedure which I suppose I should mention."

" What's that?"

" Simply, don't forget to read through your own essays. The words you have written during the school year naturally stick in your memory. If you read them just before the exam. you will be able to write coherently on the subjects concerned."

" But suppose none of those subjects appears on the paper."

" Then you fall back on that book of popular modern essays."

" And suppose none of those subjects appears."

" I feel sorry for you. But, frankly, I don't believe such a situation would arise. Still, we'll put it to the test. As our book of modern essays we'll take *Pebbles on the Shore*. Now, does anyone possess an examination paper?"

" I might be able to find one," said Roger. " Shall I go and look for it? It may take about five minutes to unearth."

" Please do," the Expert replied. " All this talk about School Certificate isn't so vital to you. I shall be chatting about Sixth Form and University work some other night."

So Roger departed to seek his exam. paper.

" While he's out," began the Expert, " I'll give you the benefit of my personal experience on this point. When I took my School Certificate——" (Alice was by this time quite used to the Expert's ' When I was in Poona ' manner) " I spent the evening before the English Language paper reading *Pebbles on the Shore*. Now, on the next day one of the essay subjects was ' The Influence of Environment on Town and

Country dwellers respectively '. Now, many candidates would have turned tail at the sight of the long words. But not so me!''

"*But not so me*," repeated Alice to herself: "of all the boastful people I've ever met!''

Angela interrupted Alice's thought by asking the Expert: "But surely A. G. Gardiner hadn't written any essays on ' The Influence of Environment ' or whatever it was.''

"Not under such a presumptuous title," the Expert replied; "but there was one of his essays that I had read the night before which provided my material. I happened to remember just one or two significant sentences.''

"Which essay was it?" inquired Alice.

"' On Pleasant Sounds.' It wouldn't seem to fit in, but it did.''

"Well, it certainly seems a pleasant way of tackling an exam.," said Alice.

"It is," replied the Expert. "Try it!''

CHAPTER THREE

SHINING IN HIGHER EDUCATION

" THAT'S all very interesting," said Roger, " but you're not flying quite high enough for me. I'm concerned with Sixth-form study and then University work. How does your vaunted essay formula satisfy Advanced G.C.E. needs?"

" Very nicely, thanks," returned the Expert. " It's *more* useful in higher education than in the School Certificate or Fifth-form standard. Both in the Sixth form and at the University you'll find the essay vital—particularly in the arts subjects. I can't discuss the scientific side because I'm limited to my own experience."

" I'm sure you're right," said Barbara. " I've noticed that the University entrance exams. usually demand an English essay, even if you propose to study maths. or physics."

" Thank you, Barbara," the Expert replied. " But first I'd like to discuss Sixth-form public exams. First of all, there's the English Language paper. And even the Scholarship English Literature paper can be compared to the Ordinary Level English language."

" Only the paper's a lot harder," said Barbara.

" The paper's a lot easier," broke in the Expert. " The scope—the choice—is wide, almost unlimited. The essay questions are as general as can be. As for the interpretation, you can ' waffle ' on anything you like. As you can write hard and fast for three hours—and write in good English—you're all set for the first instalment of the Scholarship cheque. It's been said of our modern examination system that it's the journalists' paradise. It's solemn truth. Show your versatility and speed, and disregard *thought*. You've got to write at a sprint, and not worry if your thoughts trail limply behind. On, on and on. Exams. are races. Maths. exams. are brain races; arts exams. test your flying fingers. If your brain flies, too, all the better. Maybe you've been advised at some time to allot yourself ten minutes to decide which questions to do, and another ten minutes at the end to read through your work. DON'T DO IT! It's a criminal waste of time. Spot an essay question that you can do, and get on with it. You don't even need to bother to read your paper through. Don't forget, it's a race, and as soon as the pistol goes you must be off. We'll suppose it's a history paper; you have to answer four essay questions in three hours. Louis the Fourteenth is a subject you know perfectly. You spot the question on the old josser. Without any more ado, you're on your way. This method inspires you with confidence. You're on the tide of success, and you're using similar phrases to those you learned so carefully.''

'' But what if there were four other questions on the paper that were better known to you?'' asked Angela. '' Surely it's risky to charge blindly into the paper, like a mad bull.''

'' Not at all. You see, suppose there *were* four other questions that you could answer. That would mean that there were in all *five* suitable essays, while only four are needed. This would probably set you thinking over the paper and wondering which four should be done. Time is lost that way: time and marks. You may be like Buridan's ass, that starved between two bundles of hay—because he couldn't make up his mind which to eat first. After all, whatever the paper asked elsewhere, you were in any case going to do the Louis XIV question, so it's best to get on with it.''

'' That sounds all right,'' Roger began, '' but that's when you have five questions that you are able to answer and you simply have to choose four. But suppose there were only *three* questions that you could answer.''

'' In that case my tip of ' dashing into the paper ' is better than ever. You spot the question you can do well. At once you have confidence. You write and write. You are on the crest of a wave. If, instead of dashing down your well-prepared answer at once, you had looked through the paper, you would have been discouraged to see that there were only three questions that you could answer well. Your morale would have been low. The thought that 'I'm one question short' would run at the back of your mind, putting you off your work.''

'' I see,'' said Roger. '' Where ignorance is bliss, eh?''

'' Yes,'' returned the Expert. '' You need to avoid panic and worry. And it's not so disturbing finding that you have a difficult last essay when you have good solid answers behind you. So in any examination I used to dive straight into the paper and write, write, write. After fifteen or twenty minutes of break-neck writing my brain—and fingers—would need a moment's rest. Only *then* would come my glance at the whole paper. Thus no time was lost.''

'' But if *I* wrote at full speed for three hours,'' said Angela, '' I'd be tired out.''

'' So would we all,'' replied the Expert: '' mentally and physically. Back and fingers ache. Brains become muddled. But, after all, exams. *aren't* easy, and if you're after high marks, they demand extremely hard work. My methods show you how to avoid a lot of grind in preparation, but if you want to succeed in the exam. itself, you must be ready for three hours' hard writing. After all, an examination is not a game of kiss-in-the-ring. An exam.'s a war with a thousand rivals and expert examiners who will not be deceived. It's a cruel war, too, with little sympathy for the unfortunate. There's no quarter for the candidate who is off-colour or who breaks his fountain-pen or gets all the ' wrong ' questions. You've got to be tough—and lucky!''

'' Well, I don't dislike examinations,'' said Roger. '' Pitting my wits against the examiners and all that, you know. I don't object to a few hectic hours in the exam. room, if only you can advise me how to carry out what you just claimed. You said you could avoid a lot of grind in preparing for the paper. How?''

'' That varies from paper to paper. Let's continue with our ' G.C.E. Advanced Level History ' example, shall we? Much that I say applies to other subjects, of course.''

'' O.K. Go ahead!''

'' First, I must stress that it's an all-essay paper. You have three hours in which to write four essays on subjects selected from ten questions. These ten questions will cover nearly all the syllabus which schools should have studied during the preceding year. Many schools deal with the entire syllabus, or with as much of it as is possible in a single year. Thus pupils receive lectures and notes dealing with *ten* main topics, whereas only *four* answers will be required in the examination. Because of this, the student should decide as soon as possible in the year that he will work hard at a certain *four* (or, for safety, *five*) topics. The other subjects he will leave alone—as far as his teachers will let him! In this way the sensible student will cut out almost half the amount of work that will be undertaken by less practical rivals."

" I don't quite agree," Roger maintained. " If you study the complete syllabus superficially you have a very good chance of finding four questions in the examinations."

" That's true," rejoined the Expert. " But those four questions that you can do must necessarily be the four easiest and most popular questions, since you can only study your entire syllabus *superficially*. Because these are four simple questions, you have to reach a very high standard to gain an above-average mark. Since you have only studied the syllabus superficially, you won't reach that high standard. You may reach an average standard, but, as the subject is so popular, you will tend to receive a low mark."

Here Barbara broke in:

" We're always being told that education aims to provide us with a sound general knowledge of everything, not just to turn out good examination results. Surely the aim of learning history in a Sixth form is to become a *historian*, not just a character who can pass exams. by some work-dodging system."

" That sounds very noble, Barbara, and it's very true," the Expert replied. " The only snag is that examinations exist. You may wish to be a historian, but you can't even start to be a historian if you fail your History exam. You can know as much History as Macaulay knew, but it's no use unless you can put it down in an exam. answer. Which raises my next point."

" Another time-saver?" queried Angela.

" It ought to be," said the Expert. " The new rule is:

C

' Never read or learn anything that you cannot possibly use in your examination answers.' Carried to extremes, that rule would read: ' Never read or learn anything that you will not use in your examination answer.' That is the ideal. It is not absolutely practical, but one should approach it as closely as possible."

" That seems silly!   After all, you must read widely."

" It's my view that most serious students read *too* widely, or that they read too aimlessly. For instance, we'll suppose that students are working for an Economic History paper, and that there is almost certain to be a question on the development of roads during the eighteenth century. That means that in the examination the candidate will have to write for some forty minutes about roads. Teachers usually present their pupils with some facts about roads. These notes taken in class are never enough for an exam.; they may be enough in quantity, but they are usually the basic, necessary facts. These you are expected to know, and examiners will give you little credit for stating them. If you gained a football trial with Arsenal, you wouldn't expect special consideration because you knew where to stand for the kick-off, or that when the ball goes off the field a throw-in follows. The football selectors know you know those things, or you wouldn't be on the field. The examiners know you know those facts given by the average teacher in the average set of notes, or you wouldn't be answering the paper. No doubt examiners mark many ' essays ' that are mere recitals of these basic facts. If these facts were correctly stated and well-arranged, a low pass mark would probably result. If these were incomplete (because the student had not known them well enough to write hard throughout the forty-five minutes, or because he was unaware that exams. are races), a pass would be less likely. Thus, quite justly, the mere reproduction of generally known facts brings poor results. These facts must be supplemented by facts of your own."

" And where do you get those, if not from books?" said Roger. " You must read widely."

" Yes. You must read widely. Many earnest students do. They read lots of thick, weighty volumes. They summarise nine-hundred-page books. They deserve highest examination marks, but they may not get them. They have worked hard, but their labour has often been misdirected.''

" Then how can *I* hope to succeed?'' asked Roger: " I couldn't plough through nine-hundred-page books.''

" You don't need to,'' the Expert replied. " What's the good of reading a nine-hundred-page book? You can't write a nine-hundred-page answer in a three-hour exam.''

" You can summarise the book.''

" But what's the point? Why not use somebody's short essay on the subject, and get your ideas from that? Learn those few ideas thoroughly, so that you can reproduce them in the exam.''

" Excuse me, but you just said that the recital of basic facts was worthless. Now we hear that, because only forty minutes are allowed for an answer, it's a waste of time to explore beyond those basic facts.''

" When I said ' learn a few ideas thoroughly ' I did not mean ' learn those basic facts thoroughly '. These ' ideas ' I advocate should be more than facts; they should be based upon the facts, but be little-known quotations or high-sounding phrases that present the facts in an interesting and individual way.''

" In other words,'' said Roger, " answers should be readable; they should interest or amuse the examiner.''

" If possible, yes. And I think it *is* possible if you follow these tips.

First. Narrow the syllabus down. It should be possible to halve your year's work in this way.

Second. Having decided upon the subjects on which you will answer, select the books and chapters you intend to study.''

" How is that done?'' Roger asked.

" Your teacher will no doubt give you a bibliography of each subject, and most books also include bibliographies. Let's suppose that the subject is Modern European History, and that it is generally known that a question on, say, Russia, is set every year. There are scores of books to read. One, perhaps called by some long-winded title, is recommended by

the teacher as most exhaustive. (As it contains some eight-
hundred pages, we feel that the last letters of the teacher's
epithet might well be altered.) The student reads this book
as advised. Now, if you are wise, *you* will think twice before
committing yourself to such a time-filling task. Instead of
blindly settling down to eight-hundred pages, you will do well
to consider previous examination papers. To read eight
hundred odd pages represents a great deal of time and there
are quicker ways. You find the questions dealing with Russia
mainly deal with either Peter the Great or Catherine the
Great.

" As you approach the 1956 exam. you see that a question
on this subject is a hardy annual—as safe a banker as any in
exams. Since 1934 there has been a question on every paper,
with *two* or more in 1933, 1936, 1937, 1938 (when the Scholarship questions began), 1939, 1940 and 1941. Since the
previous year's paper included an easy, general, straightforward question on Catherine, this is unlikely to be repeated.
Catharine can be ignored, or, safer, can be cursorily studied,
in case a comparison between Peter and Catharine is de-
manded. Obviously, the possible questions on Peter and
Catharine for 1956 are very few. A straightforward account
of Peter, well-written and well-remembered, plus (if required)
a short ' twenty-minute ' general essay on Catharine will suffice. You have to write these, and if you want a high mark
they must be really readable. To write these will take you
many months—if you write them from eight-hundred-page
books. If you are practical in your approach, however, it
should take just five or six hours. Five or six hours, and you
have the final material for *one* answer, that is to say one-
quarter of your exam. paper, that is to say one-quarter of
your year's work. Even if you're taking a scholarship history
paper as well, it may easily come up in each paper, so in a
single day you will have accomplished a quarter of the year's
History."

" Gosh! " cried Angela. " But are you sure it's safe?"

" Well, in the case of the example it was, for 1946 did in
fact present students with two very easy questions on the subjects concerned. If you want to be safer, an extra hour or

two, well directed, will put you right. As I've already saved you fifty-one weeks, six days, eighteen hours, you may be able to spare a few extra moments for safety's sake."

" Sounds too easy," said Barbara.

" The five or six hours' work is hard, because it must be excellently done. It has to give the impression that you've put in a year's hard work, that you've read a lot of books, and so on."

" But how can you convey the idea that you've read a lot of books if you haven't?"

" Well, it's no harder than giving the impression that you've read a lot of books if you *have*."

" No, of course not," said Roger. " I've never seen the problem in that light. If you have read a long book—if you've spent months working with it—you still can't gain credit for it within the bounds of a forty-minute answer. You can only *say* you've read it—which anyone can do—or quote a little from it—and anyone can learn a short quotation without reading the book——"

" Five minutes against five months," commented the Expert quickly.

" Suppose you give us some idea of how to write these ' magical ' six-hour essays of yours," suggested Barbara.

" Yes, come on!" cried the others. " We've already gathered from your previous remarks that you don't get your facts from nine-hundred-page books."

" No. You cut those out for a start. If the subject is Russia, you delete books like *Russia from the Varangians to the Bolsheviks*; if it is transport, you ignore long books such as *The Story of Telford*, by Sir Alexander Gibb. This is a great book—but we aren't talking about books; we discuss sources of exam. material. You would probably *not* read any biographies, such as *Louis XIV*, *Peter the Great* or *Ark-wright*, in any event. If you wish to read such volumes for interest, it's a fine thing—but don't read them for exams."

" Then what sort of books *would* you suggest? Surely very general, elementary books are no use. We are always being told that these are too childish for H.S.C. students."

" Just what type of book do you mean?"

" Well," explained Roger, " those with only a single chapter devoted to each of these big topics. There might be only twenty pages on your subject of transport, for example."

" Yes. I know what you mean. Such books, however, can be exceedingly *valuable*—if handled correctly! "

" But how?" queried Roger. " If you were to summarise the whole chapter on transport, you'd find yourself with even less than those ' basic facts ' that you've already denounced."

" True. But a summary—in that sense—would not be the correct way to handle such a chapter. In a summary you normally aim for the meat; but I advise you to seek the little delicacies."

" You mean the neat literary phrases and quotations, of course. But will there be any in a short chapter?"

" Unless the book is advertised as in note-form, the answer is ' yes '. Most of these books are brilliantly written by leading historians, and you don't catch them turning out mere well-known dull facts and dates, even for a school text-book. These facts are always heightened by curious little deviations. A summary would normally cut out these frillings; *yours* must cherish them."

" Still, your essay answers can't be all decorations. There must be facts."

" Oh, quite. Because of this, it is best to take your lecture notes (fact) on *one* side of the page only—say the right-hand side—and keep the left for a *parallel* commentary of embellishments, usually taken from book summaries."

" Thanks for the tip," said Roger. " I get the general idea, but I'd like a few examples."

" Naturally," the Expert replied. " Suppose we return to Peter the Great, because we saw from our study of past papers that he was likely to turn up.

" Now here are some interesting facts which I read in various books, and which are not usually found in conventional accounts nor among students' examination essays.

1. When Peter travelled in foreign capitals he was a badly-mannered guest—he would walk off with anything which took his fancy.

2. Peter once worked in an English dockyard, having completely hidden his identity.

3. His widow Catharine was said to ' look best from behind '. She owned 15,000 frocks and her favourite pastime was to lie in bed while servants scratched her feet.

4. Peter insisted that those of his nobles who did no work must remain bachelors—he wanted no idle children!

5. He tortured and murdered his clever son.

" These are the sort of items that will be of use to you in examinations," said the Expert.

" I see what you mean. Brighter exam. answers, eh?" said Roger.

" Of course," the Expert replied, " you must not forget that examiners are human beings, and those who mark your essays aren't the omniscient, omnipotent gods you imagine. In fact, maybe they spit in the street!"

" I'll certainly try to make my examination essays a little more entertaining."

" Good. Examiners love humorous stuff, though it's a little risky to attempt it, as you may be guilty of would-be facetiousness and schoolboy cleverness. Examiners don't love that."

" Well, we should be able to avoid cheeky cheap remarks by taking your tip and searching the more delectable items of well-written history books for our material."

" You seem to have the idea now. I think I can leave you to it."

" There's just one more question, please," Alice said. " Does this essay formula really suit University requirements?"

" Yes, those hints should help to gain you University entrance."

" I didn't mean *entrance*," Alice objected: " I mean actual University work."

" Oh, yes. I promised to tell you something about that, didn't I?"

" Yes. Is there an accent on essays in the Universities?"

" There's a very definite one—in the liberal subjects, at

any rate. Of course, when taking a degree course you don't still write essays on subjects like ' My Favourite Holiday ', even though a general essay paper is set in most scholarship exams. for entry into a University."

" Yes, but what sort of essays are written in the University by, say, students of English?"

" Long ones," replied the Expert. " University essays have to be handed in far less frequently than Sixth-form essays. There may only be two essays per term."

" What sort of subjects?" asked Roger.

" All sorts. You can usually choose your own actual subject. Whereas at school the whole class is often asked to attempt one essay topic, at a University everybody covers a subject of his or her own, and sometimes these are discussed by small groups called essay classes."

" I suppose that as University students have so few essays to do, their work must be detailed."

" Yes, University essays entail more research than school essays, and of course a *thesis*, necessary for many degrees, is really a giant ' essay ' requiring intense study."

" I expect originality is in demand," Roger commented.

" Yes. You mustn't quote a professor's lecture back at him in an essay. It is irksome for Professor Smith to see his phrases, of which he is heartily tired, occurring in essay after essay, especially when prefixed with such remarks as ' As Doctor Johnson has it '."

" I can believe that! " Angela cried.

" There's a quotation from *Macbeth*," went on the Expert, " that sums up professors' positions in such cases:

> " ' That we but teach
> *Bloody* instructions which, being taught, return
> To plague the inventor.' "

And with that the Expert vanished.

.   .   .   .   .

" Well, Alice, do you know how to write an essay yet?" asked Roger.

" I've got a headful of ideas," Alice replied, " some fantastic and some sensible. They're all in queer-shaped pieces, like a jig-saw puzzle. Still, I suppose that's all anyone can have. Now I can have the fun of working out my ideas.''

" Yes,'' Roger added thoughtfully; '' I guess that's what writing is—' the fun of working out ideas '.''

" Yes,'' said Alice. " And perhaps I can satisfy my teacher.''

PART TWO

THE ESSAY IS THE KEY

SO HERE'S HOW TO WRITE IT

ALICE gained a lot from her magical lessons. She now has a headful of ideas—magical ideas, wonderful ideas. They're all in queer-shaped pieces, like a jig-saw puzzle. And now she's going to have fun sorting them out.

Perhaps you, like Alice, will want to hear more. You've heard that examination success does not go to the man who knows most about his subject, but to the man who knows most about examinations. You've heard that exams. are not passed by swotting—they are passed by technique.

Above all, you've learned that *essays are everything*.

And now I'm going to explain to you, in detail, the technique of writing essays.

So, with Alice, read the next chapter and—*shine in examinations*.

CHAPTER FOUR

THE ESSAY IN THE ENGLISH PAPER

STARTING IT

A FAMOUS Hollywood film director once said that he wanted to make a film that began with an earthquake and worked up to a climax. Your essay should do the same—it should begin with an earthquake. Its first line must hit hard.

You must open with zest and snap and zip. Your first sentence must have the fierceness of a flash of lightning, the surprise value of a blitzkrieg. It must amaze, astound, awake its reader. It must have force.

It must not resemble the following example, which is a typical opening for an essay on the subject: " My Home Town."

MY HOME TOWN

" I do not think many people will find my home town of great interest to them, as it is not a very wonderful town, but as I have to write something about my home town, I must ask you to bear with me while I tell you something about the town, if indeed one can rightly call it a town, so I must apologise for my efforts . . . etc."

The above opening is bad. It is bad because it is weak. It is too apologetic and nervous. It lacks confidence. Its author says that he does not think that his essay will be very interesting—so our reaction is: " Well, if the writer doesn't think that his essay's interesting, why the heck should he expect *us* to read it?"

The author who opens an essay in that way is rather like a dentist who says to us: " Well, sit down in the chair, please, and I'll try not to hurt you, but I expect I will, because I've never taken any teeth out before and I'm terribly worried and I've got a bad headache and I can't concentrate."

If a dentist approached his patients like that he wouldn't make them very happy, would he? Similarly, the *essayist* cannot commence with uncertainty and nervousness. In his very opening he must hit his reader in the eye; grab his interest; seize the initiative. So, in your examination, open your essay in a way that immediately shocks your examiner into awareness.

Here are three typical examination essay subjects, liable to occur on any general English Language paper at any and every standard.

(A)   My Home Town.
(B)   If I Won £50,0000.
(C)   Boots.

I now give two possible openings for essays written on each of the three titles, and in each pair of openings the first will illustrate how not to begin, the second how to begin your essay.

(A) (i) " MY HOME TOWN "

" The little village of Clarkley, nestling amid the pleasant hills of Warwickshire, surrounded by leafy glades and rivulets, where birds sing sweetly from noon till eve, making it a perfect haven of rest from the mad bustle of the working world with its roar and scurry, may be truly described as my home town."

(A) (ii) " MY HOME TOWN "

" I live in a sewer."

(The *first* opening is competent enough, but is uninteresting, quiet and involved. Above all, it is slow. On the other hand, the second opening immediately seizes the imagination, and one is eager to see how the theme is developed.)

(B) (i) " IF I WON £50,000 "

" I do not think I shall ever win £50,000, but if I were lucky enough to gain this large sum I would think over very carefully what to do with it, as I would not want to spend it foolishly, and after I had thought about it I would first of all see that my father got some money, then I would see that my mother was all right, and then I would see that my sister was all right."

(B) (ii) " IF I WON £50,000 "

" First of all, I'd count it."

(The first opening is, alas!, the type of opening almost invariably produced by classes of pupils to whom I set the subject. Because of its slowness, doubtfulness and triteness of thought, it fails to command the examiner's attention. The second opening, however, at once shows the examiner that he is in contact with a vital mind. It is an honest, original opening expressed with bullet-like force because it is expressed simply *in a short simple sentence*.)

(C) (i) " BOOTS "

" There are many types of boots, such as working boots, football boots, cricket boots, army boots, etc., and they are made of leather, with toe-caps and holes for laces."

(C) (ii) " BOOTS "

" Poor soles! "

(The first opening insults the reader by telling him things which are of no interest because they are already known. The second opening is terse and snappy, and in two short words we feel a touch of life and whimsy which we hope will continue throughout the essay.)

Your opening sentence should be

    1. WITTY
    2. UNEXPECTED
    3. CONFIDENT
    4. SHORT AND SHARP.

It should NOT be

    1. DULL
    2. OBVIOUS
    3. APOLOGETIC
    4. RAMBLING AND HESITANT

.   .   .   .   .

BUILDING UPON THE OPENING

You have learned how to open your essay. Your first
sentence must have personality and individuality. And that
personality must remain as your essay develops from its
opening.

You can maintain a personal note if you avoid merely
stating facts. You should write about your feelings, your
opinions, how the subject affects you.

To illustrate this, let us consider that the subject is " The
Cinema ". One student might develop his theme in this way

THE CINEMA

" A cinema is a place where films are shown. In almost
every town there is at least one cinema. In Lancashire alone
there are 1,879 cinemas, and in every week approximately
43,000 different films are enjoyed by millions of Lancastrians.
Most cinemas contain tip-up seats. They show a variety of
films, including news-reels, detective films, comedies, Westerns,
etc. Many people frequent the cinema once or twice every
week . . ."

This information may be exhaustive; it is certainly ex-
hausting.

It is a too-heavy approach. It is absolutely impersonal.

Instead, you should aim at a frothy, amusing approach.
You could write, for instance, about one of your own visits
to the cinema, or perhaps pen some lines concerning some of
the types of person you have found among cinema audiences.
A clever little passage might follow out this idea, and run
something like this:

" What strange creatures sit in the cinema! And most of
them always seem to sit near me!

" In front of me I always seem to get the High-hat type:
the woman who wears a lofty hat with a flower that blocks my
view of Jane Russell's left toe-nail or the advert. for Spiller's
Shapes. Or else I have in front of me the Limp-neck type
(usually male) with his supporting companion (usually

female). This pair place their heads so close together that instead of watching Gregory Peck kissing Virginia Mayo, I have to watch the Limp-necked young man going one better.

" Then there is the Overgrown type—the huge, swollen, inflated barrage-balloon of a man who pushes past me and plonks his twenty stone on the seat beside me. He overflows his own seat and invades half of mine, so that I squirm in my half-seat and curse inwardly.

" Then from behind I hear a fatuous running commentary from two girls with faces like unaddressed envelopes. They inform each other of every stage of the trite obvious story being shown on the screen . . ."

And so on, and so on. Far superior to the factual approach, isn't it?

.   .   .   .   .

BE DIFFERENT

Individuality is a great thing. So try to make your essays something different from the ordinary run of things. Remember that every English teacher is looking out for something new and lively—but so often he receives a dull, conventional, trite, usual effort.

To be individual does not imply being showy or unnatural. Do not merely adopt the style of the guide-book or the style of the woman's weeklies in order to be individual. Such styles are not individual; they are used by far too many writers already.

Thus the use of stilted, unnatural language does not add personality to your work—it robs your work of personality.

" *Be different* " *does not mean* " *Be someone else* ".

Don't write that you " wander with rapture through the verdant fields on a sunlit morn " if you would tell your pal that you " like to go for a walk in the country on a sunny morning ".

Be yourself. Write in the same terms as you would use if you were talking to an intelligent friend. Don't write down all your slang and swear-words and " ers " and " you sees " —and take care in writing to avoid the " double meanings " that will always occur when you write down things that have only one meaning when spoken. But, otherwise, write as you would speak.

Be yourself. And if you think that in being yourself you will be dull—then you *are* dull. As dish-water.

CLOSING THE ESSAY

In closing the essay, aim for an ending which " rounds off " the essay. Do not leave the reader in the middle of an idea. Sum up your work by a neat, bright ending.

The best way of ending your essay is to end it with a line that reminds the reader of your opening. " Hark back " to the opening.

If you can sum up with a brilliant wisecrack, then use your very best sentence as your showplace for your showpiece. A final wisecrack—a " sting in the tail " may be a perfect ending.

DEFEAT YOUR PROBLEMS

Having read so far, you may scream at me: " This is all very fine—you tell me that if I write ' brilliant essays with bright snappy openings and individuality and personality and a wisecracking ending that gives the whole thing unity', then I will pass exams. Very true, no doubt. But what use is that to me? Because (1) *I can't spell* and (2) *I can't punctuate.*"

All right, all right, I reply. So you can't spell.

Now, don't let a little thing like that worry you. Let's look at your problem. Now, you say that you can't spell. Can you spell " cat "?

" Yes," you reply: " of course I can! I can spell most words, but a lot of longer words are very tricky—I see a word like ' separate ': I never knew whether its ' separate ' or ' seperate ', and I never know how many r's to put in ' parallel '. And words like ' phlegm ' frighten me to death."

" O.K., O.K.; you won't do very well in a spelling-bee; but you can still feel fine in your essay. In a spelling-bee you may be forced to spell words that you can't spell—but in an essay you can choose your own words."

IF YOU CAN'T SPELL

IF YOU CAN'T SPELL IT, DON'T WRITE IT.

It's as simple as that.

And as I've said all along—keep your writing simple and direct. In your essay don't use words which you wouldn't use in speech; thus, don't use words you can't spell.

If you can't spell " assistance ", say " help "; if you can't spell " help ", say " aid "—and if you can't spell " aid " . . . well, write about something you *can* spell!

Don't load your essays with long words—and never with words so long that you are in doubt about spelling them. In an essay you can choose your own words. Choose short ones.

I remember going to a Test Match at Old Trafford on a bright summer's day, and there were some hours to wait before the game began.

A gentleman with a face like a well-bred hippopotamus was sitting next to me. He spoke to me.

He said: " This preliminary period seems interminable."

I said it was a long wait.

" But I anticipate the commencement with satisfaction," he said.

I replied that it would be nice when they started.

" The climate is salubrious," he said.

I agreed that it was a fine day.

" If the participators in the combat who hail from the antipodes do not amass a gargantuan total, I opine that our fellow countrymen may be triumphant."

I said that if the Australians didn't win, England would.

Then the players came out, and the well-bred hippopotamus repaired to the bar.

He was a man of some education, yet nobody would envy his word-power.

His words were not words, but freaks. They would have been quite fitting in a dictionary, but they were too pompous at a Test Match.

It is a fine thing to have a good vocabulary, but it is wrong to use unnatural, grandiloquent, magniloquent words in your ordinary speech, or in your essay.

D

And if spelling is your problem, you are specially advised to keep your words short.

BUT I CAN'T PUNCTUATE

But you are still not happy about essay-writing. You now feel that you cannot *punctuate*. " Punctuation " terrifies you.

So I must explain it.

I must try to interest you in it.

I must ask you a question:

" What word begins with six I's?"

" Eh?" you exclaim.

Very well, I'll repeat my question. What English word begins with the letter " I " six times?

" None, so far as I know," you answer. " I know that Carmen Miranda used to sing a song that begins with six ' I 's. ' I-I-I-I-I-I like you very much ', or something. Still, there's no English word that starts like that."

Well, perhaps I have asked you an unfair question. You see, the answer is the word " wives ".

" What?" you howl. " Nonsense!" And you are quite justified. The point is that if you look at an Old English manuscript the word wives will appear written something like this " IIIIIIIES ". The strokes of the w's and v's would not usually be joined at the bottom, as they are nowadays. Of course, this made reading very difficult. How could people tell which letter was really the " i ", when every letter looked alike? Writers thought that the best way to distinguish the " i " was to put a dot over it. And that's why we all dot our " i "s to-day!

So there is no more in the dot that meets the " i " than meets the eye. Those interested in what Charles Lamb calls " the oddities of authorship " might find many more fascinating features of commas, colons and question marks.

For example, here is a piece of nonsense verse:

> " Every lady in this land
> Has twenty nails upon each hand
> Five and twenty on hands and feet
> All this is true without deceit."

Meaningless jingle?   Jabberwocky?   No.   For if we sprinkle some of those playful punctuation marks, we go from fancy to fact.

> " Every lady in this land
> Has twenty nails; upon each hand
> Five, and twenty on hand and feet."

So you see, it is true without deceit, after all!

I had no drinks the other night, but I saw some wonderful sights.

> " I saw a pig with great big horns
> I saw a cow with painful corns
> I saw a boy from the earth rise
> I saw a herb with clear brown eyes."

Am I a liar, or have you guessed it this time?   It needs a few of those dashed dots to show you that with my brown eyes I saw nothing stranger than a growing herb and a horned cow.

A writer who " stops " at the wrong time—like a lorry-driver who stops at the wrong time—can cause disaster.   The mistakes of lorry-drivers mean tragedy; but fortunately the mistakes of writers often mean comedy.

" I have brought the gramophone with me.   I rode the bus to the end of the road and carried it the rest of the way."

" Three arrows were loosed.   Two earls fell dead and the third went through his hat."

Ambiguity can do odd things, and even famous writer Charles Reade tells us of a man clearing a space and hewing it to pieces.   Wise punctuation would have improved Reade's passage, for punctuation always seeks to remove ambiguity.

Punctuation marks are tricky little devils, aren't they?   At any rate, Mark Twain did not dare meddle with them.   When he wrote his books he did not punctuate.   He simply inserted a list of the different stops in his letter to the publisher, adding " Scatter these to taste! "

But if we go much farther among these oddities of punctuation, you'll have spots before the eyes.

Perhaps you will be eager to pursue this fascinating subject by yourself.

On the other hand, you may be decidedly opposed to such a

study. You may well want a golden rule—an " *open sesame* " to solve the problem of punctuation.

And I will solve your problem.

IF YOU CAN'T PUNCTUATE IT, DON'T WRITE IT.

In other words, write in *short, simple* sentences. Then all you'll need for punctuation is a full stop at the end of every sentence. You won't need to bother with colons or semi-colons. By avoiding dependent clauses you'll not even need to worry about commas.

Keep your sentences short, and you'll reduce punctuation problems to a minimum. Fools who can't punctuate too often compose long, involved, complex sentences and display their ignorance of punctuation openly. Wise men who can't punctuate will keep sentences short.

At all times it is a good plan for inexperienced writers to keep their sentences short. I advise you never to carry a sentence beyond its natural stopping-place. If you *can* end a sentence at any point, *do*. Don't ramble on and on, like a gossipy old woman.

So your rules are:

1. KEEP WORDS SHORT.
2. KEEP SENTENCES SHORT.
3. KEEP PARAGRAPHS SHORT.

Concise, brief writing will give your work bite, punch, snap, fire, directness, force, zip, zest and life.

So use a short word rather than a long. It is more effective to shout " Help! " than to shout " Assistance ".

Also, never carry on a sentence beyond its natural conclusion. Short sentences are best.

And finally use short paragraphs. Only when a large number of sentences are very closely connected in thought should you make a long paragraph.

In fact, everything about your essay may very well be *short*. Even the essay itself can be short. It's quality that counts, not quantity.

AN EXAMPLE OF ESSAY-WRITING

Ah, well, I suppose I should give you an example of an essay that obeys the rules.

Imagine that you go into the examination-room and find the subject " Bus-conductors ". How, you may wonder, are you to deal with it.

Here is my answer; here is my suggestion for a possible method:

WHY I HATE BUS-CONDUCTORS

It all starts when you are very, very tiny. As a little boy of four you set out on a wonderful bus journey. To ride on a bus is to be one of the gods. There is so much to see—if you could only reach the window: but you are only four, and you can see nothing.

After a few moments, eager with delightful anticipation, you decide to kneel up on your seat. You do so—and find you can see the wonderland: busy crowded streets, honking motor-cars, bold advertisements and all the clash and clatter of life. You gaze, wide-eyed and thrilled. All is sheer delight.

" Off there, sonny! You'll make the seat dirty, kneeling on it like that. Hurry up and sit down properly."

It is the bus-conductor.

You grow a little older. One day, coming from school, you are feeling distinctly ill. Those green apples have probably caused the trouble. You wait for the bus, and grow greener. At last it comes, and, fortunately, you gain a seat. You thank your lucky stars.

The bus fills up. You feel better for the rest.

" Come on, son, stand up: there's a lady standing."

It is the bus-conductor.

You stand up. A woman behind remarks: " Fancy that boy not giving up his seat until he's told to!" You wish you could tell this woman that you always *do* stand up to give ladies a seat, only to-day you were feeling ill. Besides, the " lady " who has now sat down in your place is a young slip of a girl who could very well remain standing, but probably the bus conductor wants to get off with her anyway.

You grow older and bigger, but you're still half-fare. If you ask for a half the conductor doesn't believe you and

makes what he calls funny comments. Then, when you are
a year or two older, and no longer a " half-fare " passenger
and feel a real man, the conductor always offers you a " half "
—much to your embarrassment.

You grow older. You're on the bus with your girl friend.
You're in the middle of a romantic conversation. She's just
going to say " yes "—
    " FARES, PLEASE!"
It is the conductor.
To impress the girl friend, you hand the guard a pound
note. Instead of saying: " Oh, thank you very much indeed, sir. That will make my bag much lighter, thank you,"
the conductor sniffs. " 'Ave ye got no less?" he bawls.
Then he deliberately scoops out a handful of small coins, and
gives you change in tiny half-pennies. You *could* argue about
legal tender, but the conductor looks ready to murder you, so
you fill all your pockets with the jingling coins and stagger
from the bus. As you rattle on to the pavement, you half
expect someone will put a penny in your mouth, pull your tie
and wait for the jackpot.

You grow a lot older. You are middle-aged. You are
freezing in a bus-queue—waiting—waiting—waiting. You want
a 72 bus, and so, of course, three 72's career past—in the
wrong direction. In the right direction come several 70's, a
71, a 73, a 74, a 75, and two 76's. But no 72's. Then, after
you've waited ages, a whole tribe of 72's dash along together.
You make a dive for the first one. Just as you reach the
door a conductor announces " Sorry, no more!" and so you
join on to the end of a dash for the second 72. Of course, just
as you reach the second 72 it is announced as full up, and you
glare at smugly smiling people seated within the vehicle,
whom you know to have been in the queue far, far behind you.
The other 72's, seeing that two have stopped, have decided
they wouldn't be needed and have dashed past. So you continue to wait and wait . . .

You grow older still. One day you are riding on a bus,

when the conductor suddenly announces, " Has any passenger just lost half-a-crown?" You haven't, but hopefully you nod your head. " Oh, you 'ave, sir, 'ave you?" replies the conductor, " then here's a 'apenny towards it, what I found on the floor of the bus." Deceitful, these bus-conductors, aren't they?

They spend all their time saying that buses are full when there's really room for one more, or failing to stop the bus at the place you required, so that you have to walk back half-a-mile. All your life they've annoyed you, and now you're a middle-aged man they won't leave you alone. These conductors may have some difficult folk to deal with sometimes, semi-drunks, or strange old ladies, like the one who bought a return ticket off conductor Smithson the other week. He asked her what time she was coming back. " Coming back?" she echoed. " Oh, I'm not coming back!" This amazed Smithson. " Not coming back? Then why have you bought a return ticket?" The old lady smiled at the conductor and said: " Well, you see, they told me it was cheaper."

Another conductor on a Manchester bus had a hard time the other day. A foreigner asked him: " Pliss, how mooch ees it to go to Oxford Road?"

" That's a long road," replied the conductor. " What part do you want?"

The foreigner didn't seem to understand this, and asked again: " How much?"

Conductor: " I don't know WHAT PART you want!"

Foreigner: " Oxford Road! How much?"

" WHAT PART?"

The foreigner looked amazed. " One pound?" he echoed, and fainted.

But you grow older, and you still don't like bus-conductors, until one day you are travelling near the sea on a bus, when suddenly the vehicle is out of control, careers off the road towards the cliffs.

" Do something," you howl to the conductor.

" Yes, sir," he replies. " I'll change the destination indicator!"

Needless to say, you never grow any older.

But your ghost hates bus-conductors!

. . . . .

THE RULES OBEYED

Did you notice how that " Bus-conductor " essay obeyed our rules?

The opening sentence was short. In fact most of the sentences were short, thus punctuation problems were few.

The individual words were natural; none was so long or rare that it presented spelling difficulties.

The mood was bright, humorous and personal. Nothing was stodgy nor dully factual.

It was an individual piece of work, different from the average " run of the mill " essay.

Its ending was snappy—and it vividly recalled the title, the main theme of the essay. It was humorous in itself.

. . . . .

Go thou and do likewise!

CHAPTER FIVE

THE ESSAY IN EXAMINATIONS

IT'S SO IMPORTANT

You've now heard all about essay-writing for an English Language examination.

In the English essay on a general paper you must show individuality, personality and style: facts, we have said, are not vitally important, but must be accurate, though a factual stodginess is fatal.

But now we turn to the examination in History or Geography or Economics or General Knowledge or English Literature, where essays are still required, but where the facts are more important. In these subjects vague woolly writing—however beautiful—is not in demand.

You may wonder how to tackle these essays.

Your method of attack will depend mainly upon the standard of the examination, and we can break our examinations into two main groups, (1) G.C.E. Ordinary Level and standards below, and (2) exams. of higher standard than G.C.E. Ordinary Level. Let's examine these two groups, and our approach to the essays at each standard.

(1) EXAMINATION OF, OR BELOW, G.E.C. ORDINARY LEVEL STANDARD

Essays are important, but hardly any of the subjects contain essay-type questions *alone*. Usually there are plenty of questions of the " snap ", " question-and-answer ", quiz variety —you either know the answer or you don't, and it's very difficult to fool the examiners if you don't know your facts.

Nevertheless there are plenty of essay questions, but these require comparatively short answers, and there is often no room to give more than the basic facts. In such subjects as History and General Knowledge there is scope for originality and clever writing. You will improve your chances considerably if you obey the rules given in the previous chapter.

I cannot stress too highly that even in this type of paper the man who can write well—i.e. can spell, can punctuate, can form paragraphs, can set out his work neatly, and can show logical thought in a natural simple direct style—will shine. He will always beat the better-read rival who cannot express himself.

Knowledge of your subject is less valuable than knowledge of the art of self-expression.

So obey the rules already given—your success will soar.

Remember that knowledge of essay-writing is of importance in many papers. To prove this point I am listing the subjects set by the Northern Universities Joint Matriculation Board in 1951 for G.C.E. Ordinary Level, with comments on the essay content of each paper.

1. General Paper. All essay.
2. English Language. All essay (or kindred. Essay of " two to three pages " carries 50 marks out of the 148; the other questions include summaries; " putting poetry into own words ", etc., in which essay knowledge vital).
3. English Literature. All essay (or kindred. Section 1—appreciation of passages from set books, etc.—demands clever expression, and answers should be regarded as " short essays "; Section 2 consists of three " long " essays).
4. History. All essay. (Six questions to be answered; at least three must (and, all six may) be essays.)
5. Geography. Part essay. (Geographical knowledge primary, but many questions demand good self-expression; e.g. describing how a peasant farmer gains a livelihood in the Western Highlands of Scotland. Good writing, spelling, punctuation vital.)
6. Economics. All essay.
7. Scripture. All essay.
8. Art. Part essay. (The paper on History and Appreciation of Art is mainly an *essay* paper; on other papers

some questions request a drawing *and a written description*; others are straightforward *essays*.)

9. Music. Part essay. (Essay-writing helps in such questions as that which asks candidates to recount briefly the circumstances which led Handel to abandon the writing of operas, etc.)

10. Greek and Roman Literature In Translation. All essay (or kindred. Section 1 demands short answers in *continuous prose*; Section 2 is all *essay*).

11. Greek. Part essay. (Paper 1 awards 70 of its 161 marks for Greek–English translation, much helped by good command of *English*. Paper 2 (unprepared translation) is *all* Greek–English translation. Paper 2 (Set Books) is mainly translation into English (English expression vital) or straightforward descriptions (English essays).)

12. Latin. English expression vital. (Two-thirds of the marks for *Latin–English* translation.)

13. French. English expression vital.

14. German. English expression vital.

15. Spanish. English expression vital.

16. Physics. English expression helps. (Slight English content, but you must *describe* experiments, *explain* phenomena, etc., requiring command of English.)

17. Chemistry. English expression helps. (As Physics.)

18. Physics with Chemistry. English expression helps. (As above.)

19. Botany. English expression helps. (As above.)

20. Biology. English expression vital. (Large number of written answers required (e.g. describe the workings of the mammalian heart and the course of the blood working through it); demands fluent written English from you—unless you want to make the ridiculous needless effort of learning parrot-wise every technical detail.)

21. General Science. English expression vital. (As above.)

22. Physiology. All essay.

23. Handicraft. English expression helps. (Descriptions to be written; methods to be stated. You may be

able to make a wonderful wooden cigarette-box, but
you are unable to describe your procedure in writing,
you will fail the exam.)

24. Metalwork. English expression helps. (As above.)
25. Practical Cookery. Slight. (Even for a " practical "
exam., half an hour is allowed for a written plan.)
26. Commercial Subjects. Part essay. (Some essay-type
answers.)
27. Shorthand. English expression vital.
28. Mechanical Science. English expression helps. (Section B—90 marks out of 300 requires descriptions,
hence some command of English.)
29. Needlework. Nil.
30. Machine Drawing. Nil.
31. Mathematics. Nil.

THE ALL-IMPORTANT ESSAY

From the list I have just quoted you will see how absolutely
vital the essay is. Out of the thirty-one subjects, only three
exclude need for ability to write English. Of the three exceptions, two are the rare and uncommon Needlework and
Machine Drawing.

Eight subjects have " all essay " examination papers.
Thus you could easily gain a valuable G.C.E., giving you
qualifications equal to professional prelims., by writing
nothing but essays!

8 subjects have papers that are all-essay.
5   ,,   ,,   ,,   ,,   ,, part-essay.

Thus essays enter into almost half the papers. Of the remainder, in

7 subjects English expression helps.
6 subjects English expression is *vital*.

So if you learn English Language well, it does not merely
enable you to pass English Language. It enables you to pass
English Language; English Literature; General Paper; History; Geography; Economics; Scripture; Art; Music; Greek and
Roman Literature in Translation; Greek; Latin; French;

Physics; German; Spanish; Physics with Chemistry; Chemistry; Botany; Biology; General Science; Physiology; Handicraft; Metalwork; Domestic Subjects; Cookery; Commercial Subjects and Book-keeping; Shorthand and Mechanical Science.

So it's easy to see that study of English Language is a remarkably good investment. And in the subject of English Language, the study of the essay is most important.

I hope you agree with my theory of the importance of the essay. Bear it in mind, for it has never been propounded and published before.

(2) EXAMINATIONS BEYOND G.C.E. ORDINARY STANDARD

If the essay content of exams. at G.C.E. Ordinary Level was great, it grows immensely greater in more advanced exams. Consider, for instance, the Scholarship papers set by the Universities.

We find that the History paper (which at Ordinary Level was " part-essay ") is now " all-essay ". Geography ceases to be an affair of many maps and a few essays to become *another all-essay paper*. The Art examination needs more *written* descriptions and fewer pictorial ones. Music examinations demand *long essays* on such things as the history of variations or the evolution of opera. Scripture and Economics, previously all-essay papers, remain all-essay papers at Scholarship level, but *the essays must be bigger and better*. The language papers are no longer content with asking for translations and grammar—they now demand *essays* of one hour's length on such topics as " Discuss whether Spain contradicts the axiom that ' Every country gets the government it deserves ' ", or " To what extent have the results of the 1789 French Revolution been lasting?"

And so on, throughout all the subjects at Scholarship level.

The higher you go in examinations, the more vital essay-writing becomes.

So learn essay-writing early and well. It will help you for the rest of your academic life. It will be your key to success.

IT IS VITAL TO BE ABLE TO WRITE GOOD, LONG ESSAYS

ESSAYS IN ADVANCED SPECIALIST EXAMINATIONS

It is vital, especially in exams. beyond Ordinary G.C.E. level, to be able to write good long essays.

How is it done?

If you want to know, read on!

It's done by:

(1) Clever preparation (*long before the examination*) *of your material*. You should spend all your reading and writing time for a year before the exam. in finding the material you intend to use in the examination essays. Chapter Nine shows you how to gather this material, and how to note it.

(2) *Skilfully using your prepared material in the actual examination*. This may involve some clever twisting and weaving, but at all costs use your most brilliant phrases and ideas in the exam., even if you have to drag them in by the scruff of the neck.

(3) *Writing very fast in the exam., so that you get the greatest possible amount of brilliance down on paper.* When you find you have the " plum " question that you desired, waste no time. Write at lightning speed. You should know your brilliant material off by heart.

(4) *The Gentle Art of Bluff*. Most important, since in examinations the person who succeeds is not the man who can write well about something that he knows, but the man who can write brilliantly about something of which he knows nothing. I will explain the " Gentle Art of Bluff " more fully.

THE GENTLE ART OF BLUFF
or
BEING AN EXPERT WHEN YOU KNOW NOT

Let's suppose that you are attempting a University Scholarship paper in History. You have to select four questions and write lengthy answers upon each. You have found three questions which suited you; you have written three good essays. So far, out of a possible 75 per cent, you feel you have obtained about 45 marks. So far, so good—but you still need more marks. And yet all the other questions on the paper are no use to you. You have no knowledge on any of the other questions. What are you to do? Gaze blankly at the ceiling, awaiting divine inspiration? Panic madly? Sit gibbering? Hand in your papers and stalk out of the room grumpily? Throw a fit? Vomit? Despair?

No! You must do none of these. The situation is vital. There is a battle to be won. And the great weapon in your armoury is—" The Gentle Art of Bluff ".

You must " waffle ". And you must choose a good question suitable for " waffling ". So examine the three questions from which one must be chosen.

The three questions are:

1. " The Treaty of Westphalia might have been dictated by the Ghost of Richelieu." Were French influences as predominant in the settlement of 1648, as this quotation suggests?

(Not a good " waffling question "—besides, you know nothing about Richelieu or the settlement of 1648.)

2. " Mazzini and Garibaldi were right and Cavour was wrong." Discuss this theory in the light of subsequent Italian history.

(Not a good subject to waffle on—especially since you always thought that Garibaldi was a type of cheese.)

3. " The Germans have always been aggressors." Discuss this statement critically.

(Ah! A nice vague question at last. You know nothing about German history, except that you've heard of Hitler—so you've got to bluff your way through.)

Right, we'll tackle the essay using the Gentle Art of Bluff. Here's my suggestion, each point followed by an explanation of the type of Bluff used, for the benefit of non-bluffers who may wish to read and learn the noble art. Here's my effort:

"THE GERMANS HAVE ALWAYS BEEN AGGRESSORS"
Discuss this statement critically.

(Notice our first bit of flannel—we've written down the actual question. Not only does this fill up a couple of lines of the page and make my essay look longer, but it also makes the examiner think that we're going to actually deal with the question we've written down. Seeing that we've written down the title so nicely, no examiner could possibly suspect that we would ever stray from the point!—But now we commence the essay proper.)

" The Germans are the most aggressive nation in the world; they are always eager to grab land and hold on to it; they sometimes claim to be generous, but I consider they are so generous that they would throw a drowning man both ends of a rope." So spoke Lord Pritchard in the summer of 1915.

(A wonderful opening. It doesn't matter that Lord Pritchard never existed; no examiner can prove that. He is more likely to stand in wild amazement that a student should know of a historical authority whom he, as an examiner, did not know. And if the examiner should be suspicious and wish to check the quotation, he cannot even begin to look for it. After all, we haven't even claimed that the speech was recorded in a history book—that's why we said, " so *spoke* Lord Pritchard "; no examiner can claim to know every word spoken by Lord Pritchard throughout his life. And should the examiner be extremely nasty and say that there was no " Lord Pritchard " among the Landed Gentry in 1915, he still cannot exclude the possibility that the " Lord " is merely a Christian name (which is not uncommon) or the title of an American showman! As for the worthy imaginary Lord's imaginary quotation—that, too, is brilliant. We had been saving up the quip about " throwing a drowning man both ends of a rope " hoping to use it in the English paper to illustrate a simile! Yes, we'd been saving it up ever since we read the phrase in the works of " Bugs " Baer, the American comic columnist. His line was simply, "It was as helpful as throwing a drowning man both ends of a rope." Mr. Baer was not writing about Germany at all, but his quotation neatly fitted into our imaginary quote by " Lord Pritchard ". So we hope Mr. Baer will pardon Lord Pritchard for so nearly stealing his wisecrack! So that's how our essay begins. Let's repeat the opening and carry on a little further.)

" THE GERMANS HAVE ALWAYS BEEN AGGRESSORS "
Discuss this statement critically.

" The Germans are the most aggressive nation in the world; they are always eager to grab land and hold on to it; they sometimes claim to be generous, but I consider they are so generous that they would throw a drowning man both ends of a rope." So spoke Lord Pritchard in the summer of 1915.

" But was he right? Have the Germans whom we often consider to breed fairy-tale clockmakers and great musicians, really always been an aggressive nation? Are they really the most aggressive nation in the world? Is the German really more aggressive than the Italian or the Zulu; the fierce Frenchman or the rugged Russian? That is what we are to consider."

(Notice the purposeful ring of that last sentence. Again we've told the reader how firmly we intend to stick to the point. So far we've said nothing to the point. But we've said it very well, and we've said it in about three different ways, with a bit of junk about " fairy-tale clockmakers (whatever *they* are!) thrown in. So far, we're winning. Let's write some more.)

" The aggressive nature of the Germans has never been shown so amusingly as in the novel *Good-bye, Mr. Chips.* You will remember how, during the 1914–18 war, ' Mr. Chips ' was teaching Latin to a large class of boys in the South of England. One boy was translating aloud to the class. He read a few words of Latin. Just as he was about to render them in English, the crump of German bombs sent all the boys scurrying beneath their desks. A few moments later the bombers had passed and class was resumed. ' Mr. Chips ' called upon the boy to resume his interrupted translation.

E

The boy replied that the Latin which he had spoken meant, in English, ' The Germans are an uncivilised and warlike people.' Mr. Chips wisecracked something like this. ' You see, Latin isn't such a dead language after all! ' The whole class rocked with laughter.

" And so the whole nightmarish history of centuries of blood-stained German aggression was brought to mind by an anecdote in an English schoolroom."

(Now we've cleverly filled up half a page with that little joke. It wasn't a very good joke, and we didn't remember it very well—mainly because we've never read *Good-bye, Mr. Chips*. Actually we saw this joke (or something like it) in the film of *Good-bye, Mr. Chips* on one of our many visits to the cinema. Which all proves that a visit to the Odeon may often be more help in the exam. than a night with your textbook. But let's write some more.)

" Those boys would hardly have agreed with Mr. Johnson's description of the Germans as ' a much-maligned, peace-loving, faithful . . . staunch and gentlemanly race '."

(We brilliantly linked up our " Mr. Chips " joke with this new paragraph, in which we appear to give a genuine quotation from a historical authority. But our friend " Johnson " is, alas, imaginary! We have called him " Johnson " because a facile reference to an eminent historian by his surname alone suggests that we are on intimate terms with all our authorities! We allude to the fellow simply as " Johnson " because we know whom *we* mean by " Johnson ", and we damn well expect the examiner to know whom we mean! We also simply call him " Johnson " because if we said he was " Professor Gilbert F. Johnson, Professor of European History at the University of South Carolina ", then the nasty examiner might check the quotation and find no quotation and—worse —no " Professor Gilbert F. Johnson ".)

" Johnson's view of the Germans is an unfamiliar one to Englishmen, who have been brought up to regard the Germans as hated devils, but it is worthy of discussion."

(We seem to be showing both sides of the question now! Examiners will applaud our " fair-mindedness " and adult approach to the subject.   Always remember that it is the mark of an expert scholar, when asked to decide between two discordant views on any academic point, *to hedge!*   Let's hedge some more!)

" But the English, of all nations, are likely to accuse the Germans of ' aggression ' and eternal militarism because they, after all, enjoy a Parliamentary experience and maturity second to none.   As Churchill has said " When *heads* roll in Europe . . . a *football* rolls in London."

(Patriotic splurge always goes down well.   Churchill is always safe to quote because he says so much that nobody would be able to deny that he ever made the remark just attributed to him.   Perhaps that remark hasn't got the true Churchillian ring—but it's the best we can think of on the spur of the moment in the middle of an examination.   And don't those three dots make an imaginary quotation seem authentic? It looks as though we know the whole passage and could have quoted the whole lot, but decided it would be more effective to cut some out.   Those mid-quotation dots are invaluable. No imaginary quotation should be without them.)

" Englishmen have always been temperamentally quieter and more peace-loving than the Germans."

(This sentence takes us right off the point—but it's done cleverly, the idea being to introduce two anecdotes that we've thought of, neither of which has anything to do with German warlikeness, but both of which have everything to do with English peacefulness.)

" We recall, for instance, the story of the Cockney woman on the morning after one of the big London blitzes by Hitler's bombers.   A B.B.C. man was going round the areas which had been most heavily bombed.   One block of houses in the East End was completely flattened.   A woman stood on what had been her doorstep. Her house had gone. So had every other house in the area. The B.B.C. man thought to himself, ' Now I'll hear something about the German bombers—now I'll hear whether Hitler's parents were married or not!'' So he went to the woman. And what she shouted to him was unexpected: she simply yelled: ' You ain't seen my bleeding milkman round, have you?'

" That story, I feel, typifies the lack of bitterness of the English character. For that story would hardly be understood in Germany.

" The English attitude of calm was also puzzling to the Russian. In his delightful but rather outdated book *Russian Roulette* R. S. Lovelace tells in Chapter V (pages 112–113) how Tomski was sent from Russia in 1926 to incite the British strike-leaders to revolt and overthrow the British Government. He came to England, where the General Strike was in progress, and went to see the strike-leaders in Scarborough. When he got to Scarborough, to his amazement he found the strike-leaders playing the police at football, with the Chief Constable's wife kicking off! So Tomski gave up the English as a nation of madmen and returned dejected to Russia."

(The above two gags are of value, because (*a*) they are interesting, (*b*) they suggest to the examiner that we have bright, zestful minds, and are not donnish, academic swots (*c*) they suggest that we know so much about History that we know not merely the facts and figures (down to a page reference in a novel on Russia), but also all the odds and ends and anecdotes that show wide reading and a thorough knowledge of our subject. The fact that the first story was one we heard on the radio and that the second was an anecdote we intended to use if there was a question on the General Strike doesn't make our brilliance any less.)

" From these stories we must realise that we, the English, are an extremely pacifist nation. Hence, to us, it may well seem that (to quote the question) ' The Germans have always been aggressors '. But if we compare the Germans with other nations, it is hard to condemn them. The villainies of Hitler are no more terrible than the villainies of Napoleon; the conquests of Attila are no more terrible than those of William the Conqueror.   Moreover, Tacitus—eminent observer—gave a doubtless sincere account of the virtues of the early German Tribes, with their generous if disorderly freedom.   He found in the Germans not *aggression*, but a love of justice—capital crimes were brought before the suffrage of all, and there were judges appointed to each district, each of which had a hundred assessors.   Tacitus said that they alone, among barbarians, rejected polygamy; the female sex was held in honour, but never subjected to cruel tortures or too severe duties.

" It is true, I feel, to say that, in past ages almost all nations have at one time or another attempted conquest.   The whole exciting page of human history is bespattered with the blood of combat; of attack and defence; of invasion and fear of invasion.   Even countries whom we to-day consider to be peace-loving (e.g. the Scandinavian countries) have a history of cruel ravages and piratical attacks of which they might well feel guilty.

" Yes, perhaps the Germans have always been aggressors. But they are not the only ones."*

(That ends our essay.   We ended it with a final paragraph that again made it look as if we had actually dealt with the question.   Yet we used no real historical information.   We just remembered a bit of a film we had seen, a bit of a broadcast about 1940, a bit of the *Readers Digest* we once read; a

* It is not the job of a publisher to be a censor.   I do feel, however (with the author's kind permission), I ought to say a word about the previous few pages explaining the game of bluff for examiners !   Exams. are tests, often unfair and often full of tricks to catch the pupil out. Thus a case can be made out for the use of tricks to catch the examiner. A very strong argument can be used that it is the examiner's job to catch the pupil if he plays tricks.   There is an old saying that one " needs enough of the devil in one, to keep the devil off one ".   My own view is that exams. are about the most beastly test which man has yet devised, and it's time he thought out some truer method.   Thus I feel the pupil's integrity is not seriously damaged by the use of bluff when short of knowledge.

The point I want to make is rather to warn all that I think most of us would have to be awfully careful, especially in making up quotations, not to have our bluff discovered.   Few are so gifted as the author of our book !

A. G. Elliot

bit of a Latin lesson we once had; a bit about Russia, and so on.   We dressed it up in (we hope) eloquent prose (our essay-writing training was invaluable for that), and we threw in a few gentlemen as authorities who were exceptionally learned, if somewhat elusive.)

I do not claim that the above essay was a good essay.   But in the circumstances, it was the best type of attempt to make. What else can you do, when caught out in ignorance with half-an-hour to go and one question still unanswered?   You can gaze blankly at the ceiling, awaiting divine inspiration. You can panic madly.   You can sit gibbering.   You can hand in your unfinished paper and stalk grumpily from the room.   You can throw a fit.   You can vomit.   You can despair.

But the best thing you can do is make a brave effort.

The above essay suggests the way to do it.   I do not say that such an essay will gain you many marks, but it will gain you a few.   Those few—which you would otherwise not have gained—may be the few extra marks that give you a distinction instead of a pass, or a pass instead of a fail.   They may alter your whole career, and your whole life.

So remember, concentrate upon the Gentle Art of Bluff.

IN EXAMINATIONS, THE MAN WHO SUCCEEDS IS NOT THE MAN WHO CAN WRITE WELL ABOUT SOMETHING THAT HE KNOWS, BUT THE MAN WHO CAN WRITE BRILLIANTLY ABOUT SOMETHING OF WHICH HE KNOWS NOTHING.

CHAPTER SIX

A HOBBY THAT HELPS

SELLING THE ESSAY

Now that you have learned something about essay-writing, you may be looking for new worlds to conquer. You may even turn shining eyes towards the Press. Your knowledge of composition is naturally centred around the essay—and you want to know where the essay can be sold.

A brusque reply would be: " It can't be sold! " So it would appear at first sight, but my experience in some ways contradicts the impression.

What are the grounds for the statement that the essay won't sell; for saying that the essay is an expression of personal opinion and therefore unwanted by editors? First, factual articles *are* most in demand, and opinions of unknowns are not.

While admitting this, I suggest that pure fact articles can be turned out like machinery parts, and the ease with which they can be written makes competition intense and sales difficult.

The young hopeful, longing for the glories of Fleet Street, usually longs for the millionaire glories. He would laugh at a schoolboy who went into a University and said to the Dean: " I want to be a Professor "! Yet he is doing the same thing to send his first-ever article to the *Daily Mail* or *Tit-Bits*.

As I said, the novice's ability lies in some schoolroom experience of the general article or essay. So you can be sure that his first manuscripts will be general articles to general papers. He's wasting his time.

" But you said general articles—essays—*would* sell," comes the reader's retort.

" Yes, they will," I repeat, " but not to *Everybody's!* "

I'll illustrate my point by a true story—my own story. The first article I ever wrote with a view to the Press dealt with

71

humorous epitaphs. It was called " Humour from the Tombs ". Confidently it was posted to *Tit-Bits*. Two days later I received a communication from Tower House. It felt a little heavy for a ten guinea cheque!

Out went " Humour from the Tombs ", but the *laugh* was on me. *Answers* provided a curt " answer " to my pompous enquiries, and I tried several other general markets chosen from *The Writers and Artists Year Book*. Fortunately I had the confidence to peg away, but the battery of rejections made me almost peg out.

Now I know my folly. " Humour from the Tombs " has sold ever so many times, in ever so many guises. It has always been an essay—a general article—but it has always had a *particular* slant. Illustrated by Warwickshire epitaphs it sold to the *Warwickshire Journal*; with a Cambridgeshire slant it appeared in the *Cambridge Magazine*; *The Norfolker* accepted another version, and so on, and so on.

" But those magazines wouldn't pay you as much as *Tit-Bits*! " retorts the " guinea-pig ".

No! But the pay was better than a rejection-slip.

If you wish to write about dwarfs, or pig-faced women, or wild men, or anything else, *don't* compose a general essay on *Dwarfs* or *Wild Men* and send it to half-a-dozen general markets. Instead, write with a view to one particular modest periodical. If you don't fancy writing and typing an article just for one paper, drop a line to the editor first.

I commenced this survey by saying that there *was* a market for the " essay ", and then half-contradicted myself by advocating a particular slant. Now I propose to mention cases where general articles may be preferred to those with the particular slant.

When I heard of the paper *The Instructor*, for the " Home Handyman ", I, like most people with literary leanings, said to myself: " Not for me." I couldn't teach anyone how to make a wardrobe or paper a room. In fact, if I believed in Hell, it would be a place fitted with chisels, mallets, hammers, wood, chisels, mallets, hammers, wood, chisels, mallets, hammers, wood and more chisels, mallets, hammers and wood. How could I write for *The Instructor*?

Get hold of someone else's book and copy from it? No, thanks. It would be a very dull way of spending an hour, and you wouldn't catch me writing about chisels, mallets, hammers, or wood—not for *five hundred* guineas! I like to enjoy my work, and I write for pleasure, like most of the people who are reading this book.

How, then, could I write for *The Instructor*? I have already stressed the advantage of writing from personal experience, and yet I had little of expert home handy work. Then the idea came. I had learned Handicraft—woodwork— at school.

I enjoyed writing that article. It was called " Letter from Tubbs Minor ". Full of mis-spellings, it told of the little lad's woodwork experience. It was meant to be humorous, and although it wasn't very brilliant, the editor said thanks for the article and I said thanks for the cheque.

It had been a jolly, general article that anyone could write and would love to write. I sold it because I was not put off by the phrase " *instructional* " articles required of the " how to do it " variety.

The word " psychological " is frightening to the layman also. Seeing that a certain editor required " articles on all aspects of psychology ", I might easily have said: " I know nothing about *any* ' ologies '." Fortunately, I saw an advertisement which read: " Do you know that everything you do borders on psychology?" Paraphrasing this as " Every article you write borders on a psychological article ", I looked through my recent work. I came across an *essay*—a general essay like those that Robert Lynd writes. The title read " Strong Men are Silent " and it demonstrated the way in which our bodily characteristics affect our mind. Giants are too much in the public eye, so they are usually quiet and modest; stout men don't rush round chasing the rainbows of life, and so they tend to be jolly and contented; deformed men are likely to show bitterness, and so on. The essay was submitted unaltered and it was accepted to appear as light popular relief alongside graver psychological matter.

I repeat that this article was an essay. The essay will, *will*, sell.

"Strong Men are Silent" was followed by another essay " Lots in a Name ", showing that our names, like our bodies, affected our *psyches* or minds. This was also accepted.

Those, then, are examples of general essays selling in seemingly specialised markets. This should prove that there *are* openings for essays. It should also show that one must not be dismayed by an unfamiliar subject once he hears that an editor actually *needs* manuscripts.

I don't want to give the impression that the writing of articles which people will *buy* is easy work. It isn't easy work, though, like most things, it's easy if you enjoy doing it. Application—practice—yes, they are needed. You often hear people say: " I *wish* I could play the piano like you can, John." John probably feels like retorting: " Do you wish you could practise three hours every night for years? If you do wish to play like me, get on with the job." You see, there is no fairy-godmother who gives you Chopin's ability to compose *just for wishing*.

In a recent broadcast boxing commentary the commentator cried again and again: " It's a display of unbelievable courage! Where this boy gets his stamina from I really don't know."

I know; *you* know; the commentator really knew. The fighter got it from running round streets every morning, punching away for years at shadows, meeting all-comers in a dowdy boxing-booth.

It's the same with writing. It's fun, and it's best not to do more than you want to do. But if you want to be an immortal, don't wish you could be. Instead, listen to this story.

A guest was sitting facing the window. The host saw that the guest seemed more worried than everyone else. " Anything troubling you?" asked the host. " Well, in the garden," began the worried one, " I can see a hand endlessly writing—on and on and on—page after page—it never stops." The host was sorry that the hand was unnerving his guest and he suggested that they changed seats. The host accordingly sat opposite the window. He watched the hand and peeped to see the face. It was a large face. It belonged to Sir Walter Scott.

Essays will sell. They must be good ones, because everyone can write them and the fight is intense. A particular market should be in mind; after all, you wouldn't play billiards and say, " I'll just hit my ball and not try for anything. I may be lucky." Nor would you say: " There are five scoring shots on the table; I'll try for them all at once." Success wouldn't attend you.

You want to know how to write and present your essay? Obviously, it isn't within the scope of this book to offer instructions on laying-out the title-page, sending return postage, etc. These things are in too many books already, and if you haven't the knowledge yet you can easily acquire it.

Tips on the actual writing? Probably when you went to school you heard that an essay has a beginning, a middle and an end (strange, ain't it?). Well, the very beginning is the title and it matters.

The value of an engaging, fascinating or unusual title at the head of an article or on the cover of a novel is often sadly under-rated by budding authors. Yet a stimulating title is the " open sesame " to success, as it is the " shop window " of all literary work.

A would-be-purchaser who is looking hastily through a bookshop reads only the *titles* of the books on the shelves. Only a title that arouses his attention will induce him even to open any book. The same applies to the magazine or newspaper article. If the journals are read hurriedly, as they usually are, the reader skips through the pages and reads only the " headlines " until one of these strikes him as particularly clever and excites his imagination. Thus the importance of an engrossing title cannot be denied.

Good titles, however, are elusive. Many eminent writers have found insuperable difficulty in naming their works. They found that with continued practice they could turn out a thousand words in a matter of minutes, but they would rack their brains for hours to find the three or four words that would entice readers.

Even the myriad-minded Shakespeare was defeated. He would write the noblest tragedy and entitle it with the mere name of the principal character—never a name that would *attract* a reader. He would conceive the most hilarious comedy—but when a title was needed the Immortal Bard would bite his quill until at last he would admit his inability by passing the baby on to the reader with such titles as *As you Like it* or *What you Will*.

But we, writers of to-day, cannot afford to be overcome. It is our task to compose a title that will force the indifferent reader to want to know more.

Let us see how this may be accomplished.

A title that astonishes the reader is often a winner. In journals and magazines have appeared articles entitled " Bananas Can Catch Cold " and " The Mosquito's Love Call ", while there is a full-length book about " Fish That Answer the Telephone ". Such headings make scientific articles intriguing and popular.

Other subjects may have a great appeal if the title is clever. " Blackguards were once Respectable People " wittily introduces a philological study and " They're not ' *Grave*yards ' in the Midlands " contains a pun which makes an article on the humorous epitaphs of Warwickshire more readable.

How, do you ask, are we to make our titles more attractive?

To answer that question, here is a list of devices that ornament or strengthen the straightforward title.

Let us suppose you have written for a popular paper an article about the value of bee-keeping. You want a title. The first to occur to you will probably be a simple one such as " Apiaries as a Source of Profit ". Very plain and matter-of-fact, but nothing out of the ordinary. Now you can add force to your title by introducing an exclamation mark, thus " Apiaries Turned into Cash! " Also ameliorative is the query mark, " Can Apiaries be a Source of Profit? " The personal note gives emphasis; " Why Don't *You* Start an Apiary? " Strongest of all, perhaps, is the imperative— simply " Keep Bees! " You can't get more *power* into your title than that, but you can still improve it by cleverness. Rhyming titles are always appreciated. " Turn Honey into Money! " or " Bees can Please ". Alliteration is another weapon, while something snappy like " Bee for Bullion " excites just admiration. A topical element is useful, " Is

Your Apiary Really Necessary?'' Quotations are also popular and clever, especially when puns are introduced as in the title '' To Bee or not to Bee ''.

All these titles, however, make their appeal to only a small section of the community, the bee-keepers. It might be advisable to think out a title of universal appeal, e.g. '' How to Make a Fortune '', since everyone is interested in amassing a fortune but only a percentage of people are apiarians.

Your titles, like your articles, must of course suit the market for which they are intended. For example: a middle-brow article in a paper like *John O' London's Weekly* would be entitled '' What does Wordsworth Mean to the Man of To-day?'' A deeper essay on the same subject for, say *The Wind and the Rain* might be called '' An Estimation of the Value to the Modern World of Wordsworth's Philosophy '', while a light anecdotal sketch for *Tit-Bits* could be felicitously named '' What are Wordsworth's Words Worth?''

This matter of titles is far more important than it may seem, and not only from the reader's point of view. After all, the first reader is the editor, and if the title takes his fancy, he will want to pass it on.

And so, writers, please us with puzzling titles, stun us with staggering titles, riddle us with rhymes and pepper us with puns.

The end is important, too. If in the cup-tie the centre-forward beats three men then misses an open goal there is a roar of dismay. The brilliant dribble is forgotten. The curses come regardless. Endings, you see, count.

We've had the beginning and the end: what about the middle? I've previously mentioned some hints. I hope to be excused for repeating the most important, illustrating it in full.

If an editor of, say, a wrestling magazine asks for manuscripts on wrestling, don't be frightened because you don't know the short-arm-scissors from the Boston crab. Write a general essay. If you've never seen any grappling, go to see some. Write about your impressions of the wrestlers, of the crowd. A pen-picture of that type would doubtless satisfy your editor.

We might use the subject of wrestling to illustrate another vital point which really comes to the fore when writing the essay type of article. The essay article demands personal opinions, and it is very important *that these opinions tally with the editorial policy* of the periodical you have in mind. When marketing a fact article the writer is not likely to go wrong—you wouldn't send an article about the customs of ancient Lancashire to the *Fish Fryer's Gazette*. Mistakes are more likely to arise in the essay—the expression of opinion. You write a topical viewpoint of 800 words enumerating the virtues of private enterprise. You see in your reference book that the *Nottingham News* wants topical political articles of about 800 words. " Just the thing! " you exclaim, although you have never seen the newspaper. Probably the paper has a strong Left-wing bias. If so—well, it's to be hoped you've enclosed a stamped addressed envelope!

But don't let failures deter you. For journalism is a wonderful aid to study.

It's often said that modern examinations cater for journalists rather than students—so what better way for a student to prepare for his examination than by free-lance journalism?

Press-writing provides you with a hobby. It is a change from your studies, yet it helps them. It gives you practice in putting pen to paper. It teaches you to write well in your examination. It may also make you money! So have a try!

Here are the main points again:

1. WRITE FOR A PARTICULAR PAPER.
2. KEEP YOUR PERSONAL TOUCH.
3. KEEP WRITING.
4. REMEMBER, IT ALL HELPS YOUR EXAM.

PART THREE

THE EXAM'S THE THING

PRELUDE

AND HERE'S YOUR YEAR'S MASTER-PLAN

So we come to the time when I stop teaching you English, and I stop teaching you essay-writing.

From now on I am teaching you " *examinations* "!

I will teach you by fearless methods how to plan your studies at each stage of the entire year prior to the examination.

I will teach you every stage of examination technique.

I will show you how to select your best method of study. I will show you how to plan your work so that you save 75 per cent of your time. I will explain an entirely new and successful approach to note-taking. I will help you to develop cast-iron concentration and marvellous memory. I will show you the way to tackle every stage of your studies, right up to the very night before the examination. Finally I will show you how to conquer the examination itself.

Hold on to your hats! Here we go!

For I am going to teach you " examinations ".

CHAPTER SEVEN

A YEAR BEFORE THE EXAMINATION

WAYS TO STUDY

THE examination is a year away. But in one year's time you are going to take the examination. That is definite.

How are you going to study?

It all depends. You may be still at school; you may be in a University; you may be studying externally and considering a correspondence course; you may be wondering whether to pay for personal tuition; you may be considering working alone from books; you may be in doubt, needing advice upon all the various alternative methods of study so that you can choose one of these.

I shall tell you a little about each of these methods. I shall explain the advantages and disadvantages of each, and later explain how to plan your study when you know which method you are using.

1. LEARNING AT SCHOOL

If you are a pupil in a good school, you are fortunate. For you will find that you are, as it were, in a factory which exists to turn out successful examination results. Everything is planned for you. You have Specialist teachers in to teach every subject. You have a class of students working through the same course with you, providing the stimulus of competition. You have friends to discuss your work with you. You have a planned programme of work with breaks for rest, games, hobbies and holidays. You are entered, free of charge, for examinations. And you know darned well that you have got to take the exam., whether you like it or not, and that the results are going to be published and that all your friends with whom you have spent your school life are going to see those results. Hence, in addition to your normal desire

80

to pass an exam., you also have an extra spur to your personal pride if you are a member of a class.

So, if you are going to take an examination in a year's time I would advise this: —

RULE: STUDY IN CLASS

1. If you are in a class in a school, realise that you are lucky.

2. If you are not at school, then get into a night-school class, rather than work on your own.

3. If you are wondering whether to stay at school to take a higher exam., or whether to leave school, enter a job and study for the higher exam. on your own in the evenings, *then stay at school.* Only if *absolutely compelled* to leave school should you do so, and even then join an evening class rather than work on your own.

4. If you are one of those people who is shy and awkward in class, hates every minute of the class, and goes red when asked a question, then for Heaven's sake *study in a class.* You are sensitive and impressionable and you learn fast in class. Remember, people who are quiet and shy in class *thrive in examinations.* The type of pupil who is hurt by his teacher's criticisms and embarrassed by his teacher's praise is (quite obviously) going to remember every comment vividly. He is receptive. He is therefore a star pupil. So if you have an introverted, shy mentality do not let it drive you away from classrooms entirely. The very fact that you are frightened of public criticism by your teacher will ensure that you do brilliant work to avoid such criticism. So study in a class!

2. STUDYING AT A UNIVERSITY

The number of suicides among University students is alarming.

Unbalanced, uneven creatures amble awkwardly round University quadrangles.

First-class brains perch on skinny bodies.

Degrees are awarded to young men who are too shy to ask the way to the lavatory.

F

Men who know the word for coal in nineteen languages gape and stammer vacantly if asked to lay a fire.

.   .   .   .   .

Yes, University study is very difficult. You find that you are no longer helped by teachers who plan your work for you and compel you to do the right amount of work by the threat of discipline. You no longer have a class of friends engaged on exactly the same task as you at exactly the same time as you. For you must plan your own campaign, and your friends must each plan theirs, and their ways are not your ways nor are your ways their ways.

The discipline of planning your own study is enormous. The discipline of the Foreign Legion is like Butlin's Holiday Camp compared with it.

And those who are successful win their honours degrees. And those who are unsuccessful fall under the strain.

And to those who are studying at a University I shall have much to say. At the moment I just say this.

RULE: A GOOD UNIVERSITY STUDENT MUST BE A GOOD DUSTBIN-MAN.

1. What I mean, of course, is that you must be only too aware of the danger of over-education. You must counter the theoretical bias of your mind with a good deal of practical living. To some extent you can do this by joining University Societies, but in these you will still be in the atmosphere of intelligence. You will still shiver in the chilly air of abstract thought. But there is a far better way to avoid an over-intellectual bent. This involves taking yourself right out of the intellectual atmosphere in your vacations. Fortunately your holidays are long. Use them for work. But not for working at mathematical formulae or psychological theories or Latin syntax. *Work at the dustbins*—or on the milk round, or on the farms or on the buses. Yes, a good University student must be a good dustbin-man.

I am not merely theorising. I am speaking from experience. Within one week of taking the Part One examination of my B.A. I was delivering milk in my home town. Every Christmas I worked in the Post Office, loading vans or delivering mail. In each case I entered, for a few weeks, a new world. And in each case I enjoyed it.

2. And the summer vacations gave a further wonderful opening. Holiday Camps! Dapper Holiday Camp King Billy Butlin employs vast numbers of students on his camps. I went there season after season and saw the normally pensive undergraduates spending a summer of sunshine and seashore. They worked hard—they were games leaders and cheer leaders; cashiers and coffee-bar girls; kitchen porters and photographers; barmen and barmaids. In fact they did practically everything. Some were even palmists, as I was! And we all felt that it was a wonderful experience, amid the gaiety and vitality of a holiday camp. It was the perfect antidote to the musty months of study in the lofty lamp-lit libraries. For me, the vocation of palmist was a complete and delightful reversal of my University work. At college I read Anglo-Saxon; at Butlin's I read hands. At college I studied the nation's history; at Butlin's I studied the nation's future! And it was all so fascinating that I wrote a book about it called *The Modern Palmist.*

3. So, students, take on a job. Take on a practical job. Force yourself now and again to forget theories and work with certainties. Two of the finest graduates I've met knew how to do this—one spent his vacations as a barrow boy near Newcastle; the other was a labourer on the railways. They had the wisdom to occasionally turn their backs upon professors who lectured learnedly in their laboratories and to mingle with people who spat superlatively in the street.

Remember that if you are a University student your life is a frustrated one. You spend years training to be a doctor or a dentist or a teacher or a business man, and training is always frustrating because it entails a great deal of work with none of the satisfaction of actually doing the job. You feel *under supervision* all the time; you feel as though you are wearing L plates; you feel that you are ready to be a doctor or a dentist or a teacher or a business man, but you have to wade through masses of unnecessary books and courses. Yes, it is frustrating to be a doctor but have no patients; to be a teacher but have no classes; to be a business man but have no business —and that is the lot of the University student. His best remedy? Take a job whenever there's a vacation. A good University student must be a good dustbin-man.

3. STUDYING BY CORRESPONDENCE

Many students write to me and letters arrive from scores of countries throughout the world. Many readers state that they are unable to study in a class. Others attend classes and schools which do not cater exactly for the precise needs of each pupil—hence, many a student who is in a class nevertheless needs extra help in certain subjects or in all.

Such students can gain much aid from personal advice by correspondence and from correspondence courses.

In past years, since this book first appeared, a vast number of appreciative letters have left me in no doubt that for many readers the ideas and methods in this book were stimulating. Some remarkable results have been reported to me.

Many readers have sent their study problems to me, c/o Elliot Right Way Books, Kingswood, Surrey. Many of these readers continued correspondence, and with personal advice were able to score splendid examination successes.

From New Zealand a Mr. John P. writes: " I feel I owe you a letter of appreciation. I know that, but for your wonderful advice, I would never have passed the exams that I have passed. As you say in your book, your system does away with exam fears, and the number of units (marks), that I have piled up, amazes me. . . . From my point of view, I almost have my degree, and I can look forward to an interesting career, while I watch my fellows falling down by the wayside under the strain of doing $\frac{10}{10}$ of the course, while I do $\frac{4}{10}$ of the course. Thanks again. Yours sincerely—J. P."

Technique in exam-passing has been the golden road for many. Every day there is news of some such success. This applies to many types of exams—even to the most advanced ones. For instance, Mr. D. T., who wrote for the first time n despair six weeks before his B.A. examination. Quickly he received instructions and help, and a few weeks later he reported: " I am pleased to tell you that I have passed in all three of this year's degree examinations, *although I found that, in sitting them, I knew very little about the questions."*

Yes, Mr. D. T., Bachelor of Arts, is a living proof of the thesis of *The Exam Secret*—that, to shine in examinations is not a matter of knowing all about your subject. *It is a matter of examination technique.*

Mr. A. A. reports success by air letter; he had followed my special advice on essay-writing, and used the method for his History Terminal exam. He says " I benefited greatly from it . . . *I came first* with 74 per cent. I did very well in all ' reading ' subjects. It is a great surprise in our class."

Mr. J. A. R. (Plymouth) took a preliminary exam. in Engineering Mathematics a week before receiving my help— he passed by one mark. In the *final* exam., after three weeks of my help, he passed again—*with distinction.*

Successes speak for themselves. Schoolgirl Miss R. C. reports " top in Shakespeare " and adds " Thank you very much for your tuition without which I couldn't have attempted the syllabus." A University Honours man estimates that he " reduced his work and worries 50 per cent " by following his tutorial advice.

As a result of such successes, I have attempted to find the best practical advice which could be given to help readers achieve similar success and pleasure.

In this search a valuable friend was discovered, Mr. Bernard L. Calmus, the psychologist and writer. He prepared a valuable postal course, " Pass Your Exam.," intended to help students to approach the whole subject rationally and from a psychological viewpoint, bringing out all the hidden potentialities of each individual student.

This course was carefully edited to ensure that it added greatly to my own ideas and theories, without in any way merely duplicating them.

With the course Mr. Calmus has prepared 36 exercises as a guarantee of its personal application.

If you should be interested to receive fuller details of this course you are invited to make application (through D. B. Jackson) for free introductory details.

The offers made here, and again in Chapter 15, are open

to any enquirer in any country, and we hope to hear from you.

REMEMBER THE RIDDLE:

Q. WHY DON'T DUCKS EVER WRITE TO US?

A. BECAUSE THEY'RE QUACKERS!

4. STUDYING BY YOURSELF

If you are an advanced student, this is a good method. It is better for you to plan your own course than to pay an exorbitant sum to a correspondence college to do this for you. Books are not dear—if you use a public library!

But the danger is that you may be lonely. To avoid this you will try to find friends who are interested in the same work, but if your work is advanced there will be few suitable people.

Hence you may be lonely working by yourself. Also you may be barking up the wrong tree.

If you are inexperienced in study you will find it is fatal to try to plan your own work—only people of above G.C.E. standard should try it, but for very advanced students it is the fastest and the best method of study.

HE TRAVELS FARTHEST WHO TRAVELS ALONE— IF HE KNOWS THE WAY.

5. LEARNING BY PERSONAL TUITION

This is a quick, interesting, ideal way to learn. If you can find a good teacher—whom you admire—then it is worth studying under him. It may be expensive, but it should be worthwhile. But good teachers are not money grabbers. Many of them would teach for tuppence—because they enjoy it.

YOU SHOULD BENEFIT BY A TEACHER WITH THE PERSONAL TOUCH—BUT MIND HE DOESN'T TOUCH YOU FOR MUCH.

SUMMING UP

So, remember, if you're wondering about your *method* of study, it is best to join a class. Mistrust correspondence courses, but look out for good individual tuition.

And, having decided upon your course of action, enjoy doing your best to gain the greatest possible benefit from it!

CHAPTER EIGHT

LONG-TERM PLANNING

LABOUR-SAVING DEVICES

1. EXAMS. UP TO AND INCLUDING G.C.E. ORDINARY LEVEL

IF you are studying for an examination but you are not yet G.C.E. standard you must realise that you are a learner in learning. You must be largely dependent upon your teacher. You will be better following his advice than by following any plan this book can suggest.

But I do suggest one thing. Don't merely *follow* your teacher through the course. If possible, *keep ahead of him.* Go to the library and read ahead of his lessons; try to do the next exercise in the text-book! Be one up on your pals, and never, never, one behind.

This may not seem to be a labour-saving device—but believe me it makes class-work simple, sends your confidence soaring and saves you months of work. Your bit of extra effort will mean that you take everything—including the examination—in your stride. But if you once fall behind your teacher—even if it's only one day behind—you will be puzzled in your work, embarrassed in your class, overpowered by last-minute examination cramming and defeated in the examination.

So, as early as possible, get into the habit of keeping ahead. It's certain to bring success.

2. EXAMS. BEYOND G.C.E. ORDINARY LEVEL

A keen and enthusiastic student commences a brand-new course. What is his first reaction? Probably he will rush around to the shops to buy himself lots of note-books and every text-book that his teachers recommend. At the beginning of any University year students embarking on a new subject buy too many books. And in schools, too, there is the same keenness to get started on the work. Many pupils do far too much work at this stage.

You must avoid this early keenness. Enthusiasm is all very well—but it is very discouraging to work feverishly hard at the beginning of a course and then to find, a month or two later, that most of that early work was wasted.

Yet experience shows that much of the early, frenzied, new-course work is misguided. It is misguided because pupils do not have sufficient grasp of the entire course to have decided which parts of it are important and which are not.

So let your rule be:

DON'T TAKE ON ANY BIG AMOUNT OF WORK UNTIL YOU UNDERSTAND THE SCOPE OF THE SYLLABUS.

Normally it will take you some weeks to grasp the whole idea and scope of the syllabus. During this time you should *not* do detailed work on any minor parts of the syllabus; you should *not* spend good money buying every book the teacher recommends; you should simply attempt to grasp the outline of the entire course and then decide which parts of it you will study.

From that day forward, concentrate entirely upon those parts of the course which you have selected.

FIND THE MINIMUM OF WORK YOU NEED TO DO WHILE STILL BEING ABLE TO PASS THE EXAMINATION.

Find the minimum amount of study that will enable you to be just able to answer comfortably the required number of questions and study that minimum of work. Entirely ignore the remainder of the syllabus.

You can often cut your work to about one-quarter of the syllabus by this method. And having reduced your task to one-quarter of the syllabus you can really concentrate on this quarter, and ignore the other three-quarters.

Never mind what your class-mates do!

Never mind what your teacher does!

You are studying *your* syllabus—and it's a good deal easier than theirs!

AN EXAMPLE OF LABOUR-SAVING

Let's imagine you are tackling English Literature at G.C.E. Advanced Level.

The syllabus of books prescribed for study will be something like the following imaginary one:

Chaucer: *The Prologue* and *The Knight's Tale*.
Shakespeare: *Macbeth*.
Milton: *Samson Agonistes*.
Pope: *Rape of the Lock*.
Dryden: *Absalom and Achitophel*.
Johnson: *Lives of the Poets*.
Gray: *Poetical Works*.
Swift: *Gulliver's Travels*.
Lamb: *Essays of Elia*.
Wordsworth: *Poems of 1807*.
Austen: *Pride and Prejudice*.
Disraeli: *Sybil*.
Arnold: *Poetical Works*.
Dickens: *Great Expectations*.
Barrie: *Peter Pan*.
Joyce: *Ulysses*.

Now, it would be a delightful thing to study all those books. Most students will read them all—but not you. Most teachers will give lessons on them all—but not for you! Because you are going to cut down this syllabus.

To do this you must examine past examination papers. You do so. You find that the paper will be all-essay. (And knowing the contents of this little book you smile to yourself.) Moreover, there is normally a question about each book on the syllabus, but you only need to write essays upon four of them.

So you decide to study only four books, plus one reserve!

How are you to pick your five books?

It's hard to advise you, as your choice will be personal—dependent upon (*a*) what you like, and (*b*) what you know about. But I can give you one piece of sound advice.

Choose a set of books in which the study of each one will assist you in the study of the others.

For instance, from the above sixteen books choose:

1. Pope: *Rape of the Lock*.
2. Dryden: *Absalom and Achitophel*.
3. Gray: *Poetical Works*.
4. Wordsworth: *Poems of 1807*.
Reserve. Arnold: *Poetical Works*.

The above set is good because *all* are poetical works. You will never need to worry in your whole year of work about a single novel nor a single play! And everything you read will be poetry, or about poetry, and will help you with regard to all the five books. Moreover, all the books are closely connected in literary history: Pope can really only be understood fully if one reads Dryden (Pope and Dryden have a " fish-and-chips " type of partnership!); Gray was the transitional poet who links together the period of Pope with the period of Wordsworth. Thus this set of books can be studied easily and economically—there's a great saving of time and effort.

A bad choice of five books would be:

1. Chaucer: *The Prologue* and *The Knights Tale*.
2. Pope: *Rape of the Lock*.
3. Lamb: *Essays of Elia*.
4. Barrie: *Peter Pan*.
Reserve. Dickens: *Great Expectations*.

In this selection you would be forced to read very widely, because you would have to read and learn all about not only poetry, but also about the drama, the essay form and the novel! The individual set-books would not be helpful in aiding you in understanding the others. You would need to read a lot about all periods of literary history; you would need to learn to read Middle English, in order to understand Chaucer and to discover how the human mind worked in his day; you would need to study Pope and his age; then you would also have to understand the vastly different Victorian world of Dickens; you would also spend long hours considering the more modern philosophy of Barrie. Your time would be sadly full. For you would have too varied a selection of works on your plate. It is hard work forcing your mind to grasp the strange-looking words of Chaucer, the clear-cut mind of Pope, the diluted insanity of Lamb, the playful magic of Barrie and the outraged might of Dickens. It is an admirable literary training to read and enjoy such widely differing authors—*but it is bad examination technique!*

KEEPING TO YOUR LIMITED SYLLABUS

When you have limited your syllabus, keep to it! Study hard the items you have selected—and those items only.

Let's suppose that, following my advice, you have discovered that you can get through the European History paper by studying nothing except, say, French History. You must now study only French History. If you hear that there is to be a History lecture on Germany, Russia, Poland, Austria, Spain or Sweden, then *cut it*! And if you can't cut it without risking expulsion, then sit on the back row, reading a good book about French History!

CHAPTER NINE

NOTES ON NOTES

USING YOUR NOTE-BOOK

YOUR note-book should be your Bible. It should be your constant companion throughout your studies. And it should be a solid, thick, hard-backed volume.

Notes in this book must be neat. And as you may use these notes for many years, they should be made in ink.

In addition to your main note-book you should have a paper-backed exercise book for use as a jotter. You should take your jotter to all your lectures and classes. In it you should jot down all the rough notes you can. In it you can do all the rough classwork set by your instructor. But keep it quite apart from your note-book. Your jotter will contain many notes unworthy of your note-book—but the more important notes in your jotter should periodically be transferred into the permanent pages of your note-book.

In addition to a note-book and a jotter, you may find it valuable to carry a tiny pocket-book (like the normal small diary). If you always carry this book you can jot down anything which you want to remember—even if it's an idea that comes to you while you are on the bus riding to a football match, or a point that somebody makes in a friendly argument over a cup of coffee. A good student is always liable to be thinking over his studies, and a small pocket-book will enable him to insure against forgetting his bright ideas. I have often heard witty lines in films, plays and popular songs and thought that these would be valuable to quote in an English Literature paper. So out came my pocket-book, and down went the line to be remembered. Later it would be transferred to a larger note-book.

In my larger note-book I always wrote my notes in large legible handwriting, and I always left ample margins and huge spaces so that further connected notes could be added.

I wrote initially on one side of the page only, leaving each left-hand page blank for afterthoughts.

The large note-book is your own vital document. You write it in your own way to suit your own studies: it is a product of your personality. And after you have completed it you read through it many times until you know it as well as you know your own birthday. On the night before the examination, your last chance comes along. So read your note-book through again and again and again and again and again and again and again and again. Then read it through again. Read it until the very last moment before the examination.

That is the way to use a note-book.

Have it by you continually, and constantly read through it. Then, when the examination arrives, you can remember every detail of your note-book, and visualise every single page. Then you simply transfer the material from your note-book via your memory to your examination answer.

And now that you have your invaluable note-book I must tell you how to take notes in your classes.

NOTE-TAKING

1. *In a class:* Many classes are conducted by a teacher in a question-and-answer method, and normally the pupil has no time for note-taking. But it is a good plan for you to have a jotter by you to make a quick note of anything that you wish to remember. If the class is extremely active in question and answer, you might feel that it will break your attention too much if you stop listening to write down a note—if so, make your quick note of significant points immediately after the lesson in your book.

2. *In a lecture:* If the class is taught by the lecture method, it certainly helps to have your jotter with you. In fact, your jotter is essential. This does not mean that you *must* take notes—it simply means that you must be prepared to take notes. If the lecture is a dull one, and there are few new facts, striking illustrations or amusing anecdotes, you should take no notes at all. Never take notes for notes' sake. If the instructor writes important notes on the blackboard and tells you to write them down, you should do so—unless you

feel that these are of no use to *you*. Don't merely copy them like a living carbon paper! Arrange your notes in the way that seems most important to *you*. Note-taking is valuable because it is an *active* way of studying; it helps you to keep your mind on your work; it prevents day-dreaming. But keep your notes *few*. Many students buy big new note-books and take pride in writing down practically every word a lecturer utters. But this marathon task is futile. Only items that interest you should be noted; you should only make notes which will probably be of use to you in an examination. Long-winded note-taking will make your lectures uninteresting, because you will be merely carrying out a difficult dictation test, instead of catching the enthusiasm and argument of your lecturer. Note-taking may cause you to lose the thread of an argument. So beware of too great a note-taking habit.

TAKE NOTE RATHER THAN NOTES.

Pay attention to your teacher first, to your teacher second and to your teacher third—then pay attention to your notes!

WHAT TO NOTE

Many books advise students who take notes in lectures to jot down main headings to cover each new theme covered by the lecturer. This will provide a skeleton outline of the lecture.

But a skeleton lecture, like a skeleton man, is lifeless. It has very little value.

The bare bones of a lecture are bare and they are bony. And if you merely note the basic ideas of the lecture, you will only have a very superficial set of notes.

So do not write down mere headings. If the lecturer cracks a good joke which illustrates a point, then note down the joke. And use it in your examination answer! If a particular sentence which the lecturer uses happens to have a special appeal for you and helps *you* to understand the subject, note that also!

Aim to take notes of things you wish to remember, but not simply of basic facts.

Remember that you do not go to a lecture to get basic facts and figures—you go to watch the instructor's expert mind work!   He should transmit his own particular way of looking at things—his own enthusiasm—his own way of tackling his problems—his own personality.   You should try to capture these things in your notes!

NOTEWORTHY NONSENSE

A lecturer's brighter remarks, his wisecracks, his nonsense, and his stories always interest his classes.   They often also shed pleasant light upon the serious subject under review. But many students, note-taking, forget all about the anecdotes and merely jot down the dull facts.

This is foolish—for the dull facts about any subject can always be obtained; you can always find the information in dusty libraries and thick tomes.   But a lecturer's joke—vivid in its illustration—is not usually so easy to find.   So, if it's worth noting, note it.

Don't write the joke out in full in your note-book.   That's wasted effort.   A brief allusion in your note-book will suffice.

To illustrate what I mean, let us imagine that you wish to use an anecdote to show Queen Marie Antoinette's blasé and indifferent attitude to the French peasants before the French Revolution.   You intend to use the following jokes (?):

" When Marie Antoinette was in comfort and luxury her servant came to her and said, in alarm: ' Madam, Madam, the peasants are revolting!'   The Queen replied: ' Yes, my man, I know—but you'll get used to it!'

" Then the Queen heard an angry banging at the palace door, and she called her servant and said to him: ' Why are all the people rioting?'   He replied: ' Because they have no bread.'   The Queen then said: ' Then why don't they eat cake?' "

The above two anecdotes might be useful in an answer upon a question about the French Revolution, as they could illustrate the snobbishness of the French Queen and her failure to keep in touch with her people's needs and conditions.   But you would not need to write the complete stories in your note-book.   A brief note would be sufficient, as follows:

Marie Antoinette—high-handed attitude to peasants (" revolting " gag); ignorance of condition of the poor (" cake " anecdote).

If you continually review your notes, these skeletons of jokes will be quite sufficient to remind you of the anecdotes. Should you wish to use them in the exam., you can write *them* out in full.

LIGHT-HEARTED LITERATURE

Queer items of human interest, anecdotes, strange stories, vivid phrases should form many of your notes! A subject like English Literature might seem boring to many people, but it needn't be boring to you.

Let's suppose you are studying the poetry of Swinburne; it may be hard for you to find Swinburne interesting. But if you look for your notes in well-written books you'll soon skip through them to find such items as these:

1. Swinburne . . . did a war-dance on top of the hats in the hall of a London club, when he couldn't find his own—which he hadn't brought with him.

2. Swinburne . . . once wrote to Emerson to " inform " him that he was a " hoary-headed and toothless baboon ".

.   .   .   .   .

These two items alone are enough to interest us vitally in Swinburne. If we transfer these to our note-books we can easily remember them and produce them in the examination. They should interest the examiners, too.

True, they don't tell us much about Swinburne's poetry. We can read about Swinburne's work in lots of books, and hear about his rhyme-schemes and constructions until we drop asleep with boredom—but we can also read what rude things his contemporaries said about his verse. Browning called it " a fuzz of words " and Carlyle termed it " the maulings of a delirious cat ". More delightful comments for our note-book.

NOTES FROM BOOKS

Those are the sort of notes you should try to gain from the books you read. Don't spend hours struggling to read a book that doesn't interest you—find one that does. And when you

G

find it, don't just note down main points from the book—note down the little oddities that interested you. You'll easily remember them, and they'll interest others too.

Keep a special note of vivid quotations, learn them by heart and use them in the examination.

Many students writing in an Economic History paper about roads in the eighteenth century will say:

" The eighteenth-century roads were rough and rocky, and were not kept in a good state of repair."

This is a true fact, but a better sentence would be:

" The roads were rough and rocky: Arthur Young complained of being ' racked to dislocation ' over what they term ' mending '."

In other words, it is better to illustrate general trends and historical facts by unusual quotations or odd little events. Do not merely say that " early railway travel was regarded with alarm "—tell of Creevey who described his rail-trip in 1830: " It is really flying, and it is impossible to divest yourself of the notion of instant death. . . . It gave me a headache which has not left me yet. Sefton is convinced that some damnable thing must come of it. . . . I am extremely glad to have seen this miracle, but I am quite satisfied with my first achievement being my last! "

MARKING THE BOOKS

You must never simply *read* text-books; you must always *take notes* from them. For this purpose you would need to always have available (*a*) the book you are reading and (*b*) your note-book.

But you may want to read your text-book in a crowded bus or while waiting in a barber's shop, and you therefore cannot bring out a note-book; furthermore, you may find it is best simply to read the text-book without constantly having to write down things in a note-book. You, in fact, can make more progress if you simply read the text-book and underline the bits that interest you, and transfer them later to your note-book.

This involves marking the books—which, if they are your own, is ugly, and if they are library books, is anti-social.

Yet it is the best way of working, so it looks as if we must mark books.

But that does not mean that we ruin them. I have a method of my own which is neat and efficient. I do not underline a passage that I wish to note; I simply put a single faint vertical line just before the first word I want to quote and two faint vertical lines after the last word. This saves effort and time. It is neat. And, if the book is a library book, you can use an india-rubber and return the book without fear of a fine!

So try my method.

SKIPPING TO SUCCESS

So skip quickly through the books. Don't read every word. Use contents pages and indexes. And only note down the brilliant bits.

And soon you'll be noting your own brilliant success!

CHAPTER TEN

A MARVELLOUS MEMORY!

MEMORY

THE great essential of examination technique would seem to be memory. Much has been written about memory training, and methods of performing prodigious feats of memory have been explained. Many students are taught to evolve complicated mnemonics.

It is true that memory can be trained. Many magical performers of quite average intelligence have astounded the public with spectacular achievements. Some of them can memorise lists of twenty different unconnected objects, but when the average man attempts the same feat he fails hopelessly. But the stage memory man *does not remember twenty objects that are unconnected* for he has a system of building up connections.

This is how his act is performed:

He asks members of his audience at random to name any object. If the first lady says a button, then a button is number one; if the second lady says a handkerchief, that is number two; if a third person selects a lamp-shade, then a lamp-shade is number three—and so on up to twenty.

These ideas and numbers seem to be unconnected. *The memory man, therefore, has to connect them.* He connects the numbers to the objects in the following way:

Every number is not thought of as a number, but it connected with a place, e.g. number two is connected by rhyming association with zoo; number three is similarly connected with tree and number four with door. Any system of connections by association will suffice provided that each number is accounted for. My own associations are listed below:

1. John
2. Zoo
3. Tree
4. Door

5. Hive
6. Nix (by itself)
7. Heaven
8. Slate
9. Mine
10. Big Ben
11. Shower (11th hour)
12. Shelf
13. Shirt (rhymes with thirt)
14. Pour
15. Lift
16. Suit (Sweet)
17. Crinoline
18. Satan
19. Pint
20. Tent

When the objects are announced by members of the audience, the memory man does not place his object with the numbers, but visualises his objects *in situ*, i.e. in the actual place indicated in the above code.

In the examples given, object number *two* (a handkerchief) is remembered by picturing a handkerchief tied to the bars of a cage in a *zoo*; for *three* the object (namely a lamp-shade) is visualised hanging from the bough of a *tree*; similarly, if object *four* had been a pyjama-cord one would visualise a pyjama-cord draped over the handle of a *door*. The wonderful thing about this system is that it is impossible to forget anything committed to memory in this way, and that twenty objects thus associated can be retained in the visual memory without any fear of strain.

A student studying for an examination only requires to know how to associate ideas, he does not need to remember; he only needs to arrange his ideas in a memorable way.

DO NOT TRY TO REMEMBER: TRY TO FIND MEMORABLE IDEAS.

Ideas are memorable if (*a*) they are interesting, (*b*) they are directly associated with ideas you already have mastered.

So a few words on the two types of " memorable ideas ".

A. INTERESTING IDEAS

Some ideas are in themselves memorable. Here are a few examples which are memorable to me:

1. Doctor Johnson, the famous writer, would touch every post which he passed when he went down the streets of London, and he would sometimes walk back a mile to touch one if he had forgotten to touch it when he passed it.

2. A tapeworm the length of a cricket-pitch might be basking luxuriantly in the intestines of a film star.

3. The population of the world could all stand together on the Isle of Wight.

4. Thirty days hath September
   April, June and dull November.

The above four ideas are, I believe, memorable. They are memorable for various reasons, and if we can find *why* they are memorable we shall be able to understand what sort of ideas we should search for.

1. Idea Number One told us of eccentricity. It told us of the unusual behaviour of Doctor Johnson. His obsession is memorable; it is easier to remember that he ate his meals behind a screen than that he wrote *Lives of the Poets*. In the same way Alfred the Great is remembered as the man who forgot to turn over the cakes rather than as the man who translated *Consolation of Philosophy* of Boethius or who beat off numerous piratical raids of the Danes. HUMAN INTEREST MAKES IT MEMORABLE.

2. Idea Number Two told us of a tapeworm the length of a cricket-pitch basking in the intestines of a film star. This idea is expressed memorably by the concrete way in which the " abstract " idea is put over to us. If we are merely told that a tapeworm may be twenty-two yards long, this does not get home to us so forcefully as the idea of " a tapeworm the length of a cricket-pitch ". There is no factual difference between " a tapeworm twenty-two yards long " and " a tapeworm the length of a cricket-pitch "—but the pictorial image of a cricket-pitch is vivid and means much more than the abstract phrase " twenty-two yards ".

Similarly it is interesting to imagine this huge tapeworm occupying the intestine of a human being, but the clever particularisation of the human being as " a film star " makes the whole idea excitingly memorable. The whole picture is apt to disgust us too. And nothing is so memorable as something which shocks.

In the whole play of *Pygmalion* nothing was so memorable as the " shock " of the then-dreadful " not bloody likely ". Similarly the play *The Guinea Pig* owed a lot of its fame to the dramatically memorable use of the word " arse " in the first act.

Thus to be memorable an idea should come to us with " shock tactics ". The tapeworm image is rather disturbing, just as it is always disturbing to hear of parasites—especially when one reads that there are about 60,000 parasites on a common skylark! It is a shock to those of us who have always thought of a skylark as a " blithe spirit " to start thinking of it as a flying zoo.

Something which shocks you and disgusts you is easily remembered.

SHOCK MAKES IT MEMORABLE.

3. Idea Number Three: " The population of the world could all stand together on the Isle of Wight."

Memorable because it gives us a definite picture—it makes an abstract idea more concrete. If you want to remember an idea, put it in its most concrete form. For example, do not try to remember that 26 per cent of the population of Manchester died at birth in 1854; instead remember that about " one child in four died in birth a hundred years ago "; or think of it in this way: " If I had been born in 1854 I would have had only three chances in four of living."

If you can create a concrete picture of the idea you are trying to remember, you will find memory easy. Any point is best made and remembered if you give a vivid illustration of it.

Let us suppose you are a schoolboy trying to get the hang of the Law of gravitation. You read: " *Every particle of matter in the universe attracts every other particle of matter with a force or power directly proportionate to the quantity of matter in each, and decreasing as the squares of the distances which separate the particles increase.*" To you this is double Dutch. It does not inspire you to remember it easily. But you can come to see the principle far better—and remember it far better—if you begin with an illustration like this: " *Twenty-two husky Earthmen playing their usual Saturday football match on the Moon would require a field so big that the crowd would need binoculars to follow the game.*" A schoolboy reading this idea would easily remember it. He would be interested, and rather surprised by the idea. He will ask: " Why would the footballers need such a big field?" Then he could be told that the gravitational pull on the moon was much less than that on Earth because the moon is much smaller than the earth. Thus without much energy a man could jump the height of a house. With this vivid picture in his mind, the boy is interested and able to learn that " *Every particle of matter in the universe attracts every other particle of matter with a force or power directly proportionate to the quantity of matter in each, and decreasing as the squares of the distances which separate the particles increase.*" VIVID CONCRETE EXPRESSIONS MAKE IT MEMORABLE.

4. Idea Number Four: that little oft-quoted " handyman " of a poem:

" Thirty days hath September . . ."

It is used wherever English is spoken as a mnemonic to tell us at once the number of days in any month. And the jingle makes it memorable. Poetry can be useful as well as ornamental. Poetry, in fact, is often merely a memory-guide. So don't forget the plebeian side of poetry—poetry is not all long-haired long windedness, and (as Mr. Stephen Spender once said) people who try to put poetry on a pedestal only succeed in putting it on the shelf. JINGLE MAKES IT MEMORABLE.

As well as jingles of words, we sometimes find " jingles " of numbers, or, at least, groups of numbers that are easily memorable. Groups like " Whitehall 1212 " and " 999 " are easy to hold in the mind—to criminals' regret! I can always remember from the history book studied when I was nine the fact that the Danes invaded England in 789. The three consecutive numbers 7, 8, 9, still shine in the memory, even though the rest of the chapter on Saxon history is forgotten. Similarly I cannot forget that the French Revolution broke out in 1789.

When studying history you will often need to remember figures, dates and statistics. But do not try to remember whole pages of dates and entire pages of statistics. Simply choose the dates and statistics that vividly illustrate your point, and that are most memorable in themselves.

Here is an example of some statistics and information which you might find in a book on English Economic History, dealing with Farming in the Nineteenth Century.

" The Napoleonic Wars assisted farmers in many ways, but 1813 to 1837 were black years for English farming. Prices of wheat per quarter monthly in 1813 were as follows:

January	123s.
February	126s.
March	128s. 3d.
April	122s.
May	117s.
June	129s. 6d.
July	132s.
August	104s.
September	99s. 9d.
October	69s. 6d.
November	61s. 6d.
December	52s. 6d. "

Now those statistics are not worth learning *in toto*. Some students would learn them " parrot fashion "—but this would be a waste of time. There is no point in learning them all, because it is unlikely that you would quote them all in an examination, and if you did quote them it would not show any skill at history, but merely a good memory for trivia!

Moreover, it would require considerable time and effort to commit those figures to memory and to keep them in your head.

Yet certain of the figures are worth remembering because they vividly illustrate the amazing price fall after the abundant harvest of 1813.

So remember some of the figures. Do not remember them by effort, but pick out the figures that are memorable to you either because of association or because of jingle.

It needs no effort to remember the basic fact that 1813 was the black year for farming, since Number *13* is traditionally unlucky. So remember it this way:

1813 (unlucky 13) was the *unlucky* year for farmers.

Having jotted this note in your book, consider the month-by-month figures. You do not need to remember the prices for *every* month, so which figures are most memorable?

January, 123s. (Memorable—what numbers could be more memorable than 1, 2, 3, as the price for the first month.)

July, 132s. (Also memorable; the highest price reached repeats the figures of the first month but the last two digits are reversed.)

September 99s. 9d. (Most memorable—9, 9, 9, for the *ninth* month.)

November 61s. 6d. (Memorable—if you spot that this is exactly half the price of the opening January price of 123s.)

.   .   .   .   .

So now write down the information in your own note-book in the following form:

" 1813 (unlucky thirteen) was the unlucky year for English farmers. Wheat price in January was 123s. per quarter, and prices remained good until July when they reached a peak of 132s. A slump followed, and in September the price was 99s. 9d., falling to half the January price in November when the figure was only 61s. 6d."

Use the information in this form in your examination and the examiner will believe that you cannot only remember figures, but also use them intelligently to illustrate your point. He will feel that you have a great memory—but you have not taxed your memory at all; you have simply associated your ideas!

B. ASSOCIATED IDEAS

I have already said that when you study you should not try to remember, but simply find memorable ideas. Some ideas, we have seen, are memorable in themselves because human interest makes them memorable, or because shock makes them memorable, or because vivid expression makes them memorable, or because jingle makes them memorable.

Other new ideas are memorable because they are directly associated with ideas that you have previously mastered.

Because of this, every bit of knowledge you acquire not only is valuable in itself, but is also valuable in that it will enable you to understand and remember all the later facts connected with that one fact. Similarly each one of the later facts thus grasped will illumine a wide range of further facts. In this way one fact understood may well help you to understand and associate ten more, which, mastered, will each give you ten further ideas, and the resultant hundred will bear fruit tenfold. If ever you feel that it is a waste of time mastering any single point, remember the way in which knowledge expands.

You may feel, for instance, that it is rather pointless reading the play of *Macbeth*. But in your study you read a criticism of *Macbeth* which compares *Macbeth* to *Hamlet*. So you decide to understand this comparison and you visit the *Odeon* to see the film of *Hamlet*. This makes your interest grow and you find yourself reading other tragedies. You then hear mention of all Shakespeare's tragedies, and you not only see Shakespeare's plays, but also hear about the other writers of Shakespeare's time. You start to visit the theatre, and instead of always being shy and awkward when plays are mentioned, you now begin to feel yourself an authority. And your interest in plays leads you on to increased enjoyment of films and novels and poetry, until the whole world of literature lies at your feet and you sport your University degree in English!

And yet you felt that your English lesson on *Macbeth* was a waste of time!

ONE FACT MASTERED MEANS A THOUSAND ENJOYED.

.   .   .   .   .

One interest, then, expands into another. One piece of knowledge helps you to remember ten others.

And if you are interested you learn very quickly; you remember what interests and affects you.

A bachelor who gambles listens to a budget broadcast with a non-gambling family man—both hear the same figures, but the gambler remembers the tote tax figures and does not recall family allowance figures; the father knows all the new family allowances, but does not remember the betting-tax news.

In the same way you will remember new facts if you have developed your interests in the subject previously. One fact mastered means a thousand understood.

MEMORABLE MEMORY MEMOS

1. SHORT HOURS FOR LONG MEMORIES—avoid tiredness and staleness; if you stop working when you want to do more you'll never want to stop working for ever.

2. REMEMBER NUMBERS TO REMEMBER MORE NUMBERS—practice in a particular type of memorising makes that type of memorising easier, e.g. every piece of verse committed to memory makes it easier to remember every other poem you ever read!

3. DON'T BE A PARROT: remember by vivid interest; find out the full meaning, even if you have to work to master more advanced work to do so.

4. THE BEST WAY TO REMEMBER THE ALPHABET IS TO WRITE WORDS; if you want to remember any point use that point as the basis of more advanced work.

5. REMEMBER LOTS, NOT JOTS. It is proved that it's quicker to memorise a long passage as a whole, than to

master each part separately: Splitting up the passage into short parts and learning each part *appears* best because it shows us signs of progress all the time—but the less attractive method of learning the *whole* at once saves one fifth of your time!

6. BE YOUR OWN EXAMINER; constantly test yourself; review your work to know how much you've remembered. Constant review makes memory easy.

7. HAVE YOUR OWN BROADCASTING STATION; recite aloud things you want to remember; talk about them to your friends, and if you've no friends willing to listen, run your own radio station every night in bed, giving brilliant educational talks to an imaginary listening public!

8. BITS TO REMIND YOU OF LOTS; when you get the hang of a different idea (e.g. a geometrical theorem) just write down for memorising the *gist* of the idea rather than the whole thing. A few words may be enough to recall a whole lecture.

9. MNEMONICS HELP—but interest helps more. You don't need mnemonics if you really know your subject.

CHAPTER ELEVEN

CAST-IRON CONCENTRATION

CONCENTRATION

WHAT exactly is concentration? Well, concentration can be clearly defined as discipline of the mind—a complete mastery of yourself when you are in the examination room.

Concentration is necessary in all walks of life. Successful sportsmen and women, however good their natural ability, would find it impossible to reach the heights of greatness without a great deal of concentration. Our opinion concerning a Test Match cricketer who continually missed catches while fielding in the slips wouldn't be high. But cricketers who represent their country are of a high standard; they love their work, and consequently they are concentrating all the time by anticipating where the ball is likely to be hit by the opposing batsmen.

What can be done to make a student concentrate hard and without difficulty? The most important thing of course, is a natural aptitude to be able to concentrate; a lazy student will find it harder to concentrate than a keen, intelligent and hardworking student. The keen student will be ambitious to reach the top in his chosen career, and this added incentive will make him concentrate with great determination and skill.

A student should avoid over-taxing himself on one particular subject, and I strongly advise students to be interested in a variety of subjects. Whether collecting foreign stamps or painting landscapes in water-colours, hobbies develop concentration. Other interests give an added stimulant to a student's mind. Playing sport is an ideal way of refreshing oneself, for the tasks that lie ahead. Using up surplus energy in this way—apart from exercising and developing the body— also avoids over-burdening the mind and the resultant sluggishness when confronted with a difficult problem in the examination.

Try to acquaint yourself with people in all walks of life: familiarisation of people's everyday trials and tribulations give an added zest. Curiosity may have killed the cat, but curiosity (in its proper form, that is) usually results in an intelligent and hard-working student.

The individual student himself must be his sternest critic because only *he* knows whether or not he has reached the required standard he has set for himself.

Many students find the hardest part of an examination is the first glance at the test paper. If they see a question that they are not too confident about, a feeling of depression and panic sweeps over them, but normally once the examination is under way all nerves and fears are forgotten. I remember quite distinctly on one occasion I was confronted with what I thought was a very difficult algebraic problem, and I was not very confident about solving it, but by concentration and logical reasoning I was able to answer the problem satisfactorily.

It would appear, then, that the main essentials are will-power and determination to succeed at all costs; above all, concentrate harder on your weaknesses, and do not pass over a particular point until you are 100 per cent satisfied in your own mind that if a question should arise on that point you are capable of answering the question and thus earning maximum marks.

All great people in history—whether statesmen, military leaders or philosophers—have solved exceptionally difficult problems by their ability to think hard and make the correct decision. Only by deep concentration and determination have these problems been solved. Yet we see great military leaders who became over-confident (e.g. Napoleon and Hitler) who at first received so much success. All their campaigns were triumphs of strategy, but these successes led them into careless ways, and where previously their armies had triumphed they were now meeting countless defeats; the opposition seemed stronger and more forceful through over-confidence on behalf of the aggressors. So students, too, must avoid over-confidence which very often results in conceitedness. Over-confidence can be just as dangerous as lack of confidence.

Everyone should have a goal in mind. Students who hope

to make the grade in the scientific world should take as their pattern Einstein, who even at the age of seventy-four is still working on theories that have baffled mankind over the centuries. He is not deterred by past failures, but is concentrating and believing that sooner or later he shall have found one more solution that mankind might be all the greater for it.

If you have been studying hard late at night and are unable to grasp a particular point at issue, rise early the following morning and concentrate where you left off the night before and more often than not you will be able to understand that problem that had made you weary and frustrated the night before.

While learning something parrot-fashion is an unwise approach to an examination, if you go over a number of times to yourself the lesson you have just completed your mind will stand a much better chance of retaining that knowledge. If you throw mud at a wall, some of it will stick, similarly the more mud you throw at the wall the greater amount of mud that will stick.

Many students do not realise that by concentrating the memory is being trained, and thereby enabling the brain to produce maximum effort when required at the examination itself.

All students should be wary of a " couldn't care less " attitude, which appears to be very prominent in the world to-day. Do not become irritable if you do not solve a problem straight away; remember as your paragon the famous case in history of Robert Bruce, who in spite of six successive defeats by the English tried once more for the seventh time, and this time he was successful.

It cannot be over-emphasised that if you wish to reach a high standard in the world at large, it can only be obtained by very hard work and thoughtful concentration when faced with problems that may effect your whole future. Even a genius has to concentrate hard and often. Before you lies the path to success. Go to it with a will! But may fortune smile on you to help you along the hazardous path to success and happiness.

CONCENTRATED COMMENTS

1. CONCENTRATE AND WATCH YOURSELF WIN—whether it's tap-dancing or table-tennis, snooker or sword-swallowing, geography, or juggling, concentration will bring success.

2. DON'T WORRY, WORK!   Get started on that big job.   If you are tackling a job that's going to take a month, decide what you can do to-day and do it immediately.   You can't have the pip and work.

3. DON'T LET YOUR MIND WANDER—but if you find that you just cannot take in any more ideas and that your mind continues to wander, then let your body wander too. Go to the pictures or play tennis or listen to the radio. Hobbies are helpful here.

4. IF YOU CAN'T STAND THE SIGHT OF A BOOK, DON'T LOOK AT IT.   If you literally can't stand the sight of a book, or if you have nightmares about your studies, you are suffering from anxiety neurosis.   This mustn't alarm you; it's a common complaint among keen students.   It doesn't mean that you are going crazy; it just means that you've done good work and you need a rest.   One easy day should put you right!

5. WORK ACTIVELY WHEN YOU WORK—never just " read " books—always have your note-book and make notes. This ensures concentration.

6. WORK WHEN YOU WORK; PLAY WHEN YOU PLAY.   Nothing ruins concentration so much as idly " thinking about " your work.   That tires you out.   Good hard work is stimulating and refreshing and saves you from all your vague worries.

7. DON'T STRUGGLE TO CONCENTRATE ON A BOOK THAT DOESN'T INTEREST YOU—FIND ONE THAT DOES!

H

8. WORK TILL THE SMALL HOURS AND YOU'LL HAVE A SMALL BRAIN—sleep's vital, and after a good night's rest you'll find your overnight problems solving themselves.

9. TAKE NOTE RATHER THAN NOTES—in class it may help you to concentrate if you take notes, but beware of too great a note-taking habit. Unless the instructor specifically tells you to take notes, do so sparingly. Some students take so many notes that they lose the thread of the lecture—and the spirit and enthusiasm of the teacher!

CHAPTER TWELVE

THE NIGHT BEFORE THE EXAMINATION

IT is not a good plan to get drunk on the night before the examination.

Many people have advocated that a student should give himself a holiday the night before the examination, so that he will not become stale. They say it is better for him to spend the night before the exam. at the cinema or the theatre, and to forget all about his studies. But this is a very foolish doctrine.

The night before the examination is the one time when the student should *really* work. It does not matter so much if he fails to work for a month before this time—but he must work at the last minute.

This does not mean that I advise a student to work all through the night, or even late into the night before the examination. If anything, you should go to bed earlier than usual, to ensure fitness. In a mathematical or linguistic exam. it is essential to feel fit and rested. Nevertheless, although observing normal hours of sleep, you should work hard before the examination.

So let us put it this way. When the exam. becomes near you should use every available moment for working at it. Work in buses, on trains; as you walk to the bus; while you eat your dinner, and *at every odd moment when there seems to be nothing to do*. A lot of students refuse to do any last minute work, saying it will cloud their brains or make them, by struggling to remember something, forget something else. But in actual fact, notes read at the last minute before entering the examination are easily remembered, and it does not make you forget anything you knew before. Reading your notebook right until the time when you are in the examination room and are told to put your books away should be your aim.

Do not worry about straining yourself through overwork. If you are doing too much, nature will stop you.

RULE: DO NOT TELL YOURSELF IT IS TIME TO STOP WORKING, LET YOUR NERVOUS SYSTEM TELL YOU.

Many examinations are failed by those who do too little work; few are failed by those who do too much.

But remember that *quantity* of work alone is no guide to success. A little planned study is better than a lot of undirected scholarship.

If you have followed the advice of this book in the year preceding the examination, you should never have overworked. Because of this your rush of last-minute activity will not harm you. You will still be fresh and interested in your subject. Those students who work for fourteen hours a day throughout the year are the ones who will crack under the pressure of fatigue and examination nerves.

RULE: EVEN IF YOU NEVER DO MUCH WORK AT ANY OTHER TIME, MAKE SURE YOU DO A LOT JUST BEFORE THE EXAM.

CHAPTER THIRTEEN

THE BIG DAY!

THE EXAMINATION ARRIVES

THE day of the examination arrives. This is the day you've been waiting for. This is the big day, and you're going to knock those examiners for six. You've planned your study well, and you are full of confidence.

And you still have a good deal to do before the examination starts at nine o'clock.

GET OUT OF BED A LITTLE EARLIER ON THE EXAM. DAY—IF YOU PASS YOU'LL BE ABLE TO LIE IN BED FOR THE REST OF YOUR LIFE! (?)

Yes, be sure to rise early on the morning of your examination. Get out of bed fifteen or twenty minutes earlier than usual and you will avoid rush and panic. Nothing is worse than a last-minute nervous dash to the examination room. So allow yourself plenty of time to get there. If your bus journey to the exam. usually takes half an hour, allow yourself three-quarters of an hour on this day. And plan so that—even if you should miss a couple of buses and be held in conversation by the chatterbox who lives next door—you are still in the examination room at least fifteen minutes before the examination commences.

If you get out of bed extra early on your examination morning, you will find the effort well worth the sacrifice. If you pass your exam. it will enable you to get a higher post in your later life, and you'll probably belong to the class of workers who can stay in bed in the morning and think blissfully of their lower-ranking workmates who are already at the office. So, next time you feel envious of the " boss " who doesn't arrive in the office until ten o'clock in the morning, remember that he may have won this luxury by getting out of bed just twenty minutes earlier when he took one of his examinations!

SO SET OUT FOR YOUR EXAMINATION EARLY.
Make provision for all emergencies and untoward happenings.
It would be annoying if your pen ran out of ink in the middle
of the exam. But don't worry about that—simply take a
bottle of ink with you!

Don't panic because your pen-nib may break in the examination—instead, take an extra pen.

And don't forget a ruler, even if you only need it for " ruling
off " essays. Don't forget a pencil. Don't forget a bottle of
good ink, which may save you from using the lack-lustre mix-
ture that is sometimes supplied in examination rooms. And
above all, don't forget a watch. Time is vital. It's true that
the examiners may provide a clock, but you will probably
find that they have placed you in a seat from which it's awkward to see the clock. You may well have to spend valuable
seconds turning right round craning your neck to see a clock
on the wall behind you. This gyration wastes time (it's more
convenient to keep glancing at your own watch placed on the
desk in front of you) and your contortions may look suspicious
to the invigilator, who may even accuse you of attempting to
copy the paper of the chap behind you!

So take to your examination a bottle of ink, an extra pen;
a pencil, a ruler and a watch. And don't rush round your
house on the morning of the examination looking for these
items. Get them all ready on the night before the examination.

BE ALL BELT AND BRACES—ALLOW FOR EVERY
EMERGENCY.

.   .   .   .   .

Now, this is the morning of the examination. This is the
time when you must avoid examination nerves.

AVOID EXAMINATION NERVES BY KEEPING BUSY.
You can't have the pip if you are working. Besides, there's
a lot to do.

Last-minute reading of notes is most valuable. So, on the
examination morning, read your note-book while you " strap-
hang " in the bus. Read your note-book as you walk from

the bus to the examination hall. Sit down at your desk and then read your note-book. And when your pal says: " Put your note-book away; if you don't know it now, you never will ", still read your note-book. Only when the examiner finally orders you to put your note-book away should you do so.

For that note-book in a few pages has crystallised for you the entire work of a year. It reminds you of an hour's lecture you had last August; of a class you attended in September; of an evening's swotting you did under the sinking sun in April; of that long and brilliant book you read one day in May; of what Mr. Brown, that patient teacher, told you in March, of that clever idea you had last winter; of that long discussion you had with Jim before the Christmas party; of that point that you could never quite understand and that you struggled with throughout the Easter holidays; of that telling-off you received from the Headmaster; of those lessons you learned throughout the year. All the year's work is recalled by a few pages in your note-book. And the very act of merely turning over the pages is an entire refresher course. And your note-book is your personal account of the highlights of the things you wish to remember; the quotations you wish to quote to the examiner; the facts you are going to use in your answers; the illustrations that you are going to repeat in the examination.

So read your note-book until the very last moment before the examination. This revision will not only imprint every item perfectly upon your brain: it will also keep you busy and prevent you suffering from examination nerves.

Keep busily reading your note-book and you will have no time to suffer from examination nerves. Remember, you never notice ear-ache when you are running a race. Similarly, you do not suffer from examination nerves while you are busy.

. . . . .

Don't be afraid of being off-colour during the examination. If the exam. is very important, a candidate may be frightened lest he should have diarrhœa or start to vomit on the big day, thus ruining his year's work. Don't worry unduly about this: consider the chance mathematically, and if you are a normal healthy person you'll probably realise that in your whole life you have only been attacked by sudden ill-health on two or three occasions, and then only after taking liberties with your diet. Hence, the chance of being physically ill during a two-hour examination is at least a thousand to one. But if you *do* worry about this " thousand to one " chance, your very worry may cause trouble. You may in fact worry yourself into a condition of " examination nerves ". To avoid such worry, keep busy at your work, and also realise that even if you are " off-colour " for the examination *you can still pass*. In the actual examination room you will be far too occupied to worry about a slight headache or a sore throat. You will forget all about such ailments, just as you forget the blisters on your feet while you are playing an exciting soccer match, only to feel them crippling you when you walk off the field after the game.

DON'T WORRY ABOUT BEING OFF-COLOUR—IN AN EXAMINATION A MAJOR PAIN IS UNLIKELY AND A MINOR ONE UNNOTICED.

. . . . .

THE EXAMINATION ROOM

You have now arrived in the examination room. You have followed the entire study campaign described in this book, and you feel fairly confident. You have avoided last-minute panic by entering the examination room early and fully equipped with everything you need.

You have avoided examination nerves by keeping busy. You have read your note-book for the last time. You have been told to put your note-book away. You are on your own. And there will be a short wait for the paper. You might feel a little scared—but you remember to keep busy. There is probably a form to fill in; and if you write your name and full details on the front-page of your answers booklet, it will save valuable time later on.

Then at last, with pomp and circumstance, the examination papers are taken from their sealed envelopes. A few moments later is the exciting time when you see the paper. On it depends your future career.

Many schoolmasters would advise you to spend a long time reading carefully through the paper. But this is bad advice. You can't afford a lot of time, and every minute you spend reading through the paper loses you confidence. All you should look for are the vitally important instructions—i.e. find out how many questions you have to answer in the various sections. The instructions will probably be identical to those of previous years, in which case no further thought is required. Months ago you will have worked out how long a time you can spend on each answer.

So get writing quickly. Spot a question you can answer and answer it. As soon as you are in the throes of the examination you are immune from examination nerves.

EXAMS. ARE RACES—BE QUICK OFF THE MARK.

Then keep writing and working hard. You should never stop to think. Just write and write and write. If you are held up on a knotty problem, leave it, and carry on with something you are sure of. When you return to your knotty problem, you may find it as simple as sucking a lollipop.

A Rule for examination problems?—LOVE 'EM AND LEAVE 'EM. Love them if you can do them—and leave them if you can't!

WHEN YOU'VE FINISHED

By all means leave difficult problems. But never, never, never, never leave the examination room early because you've finished. If the paper lasts for two hours, stay working at it for two hours—don't leave half-an-hour early because you think you've finished. That is a suicidal waste of vital time—vital, if only for checking purposes.

And don't forget—in order to avoid finishing your paper early leave an essay question till the end. Then, if you should end early, you simply fill in the time adding a few more paragraphs to your essay.

AFTER THE PAPER

When you leave the examination room and hand in your paper you will meet all your friends outside.

" Well, Joe," they'll say: " how have you gone on?"

You may feel that you've done very well. If so, say so. Tell your friends that you are certain you've passed. Tell your friends quite boldly, for you are bolstering up your morale at the same time. They will probably be gloomy and tell you that they have " pipped for a cert ".

Then you will all discuss the paper. It is not a good plan to indulge in post-mortems, for they are usually rather disappointing. You are certain to find that you have made mistakes which you hadn't realised.

This will upset you. That upset could be dangerous to your examination nerves, but it won't be dangerous if you remember that a post-mortem *always* reveals new mistakes.

Rest assured that you have not failed your examination unless the post-mortem reveals one of the following:

1. That although you thought you had finished the paper, you really had not finished because you forgot to turn over a page.

2. That you did not attempt the correct number of questions because you misread the instructions.

3. That you completely missed the boat on a big and important question, e.g. you find you have written six pages about Charles the First when you were supposed to be writing about Charles the Fifth.

If you've followed the advice in this chapter about paying particular attention to the examination instructions, you should not have made any of the above errors.

Nevertheless hundreds of thousands of people have failed in their careers through this type of mistake.

IF YOU THINK YOU'VE PASSED, DON'T WORRY ABOUT THE MINOR ERRORS THAT THE POST-MORTEM REVEALS.

BUT IF YOU'RE NOT SURE YOU'VE PASSED

If you are not sure you've passed, then you probably have. Remember that only a small percentage of students fail.

Your chances of passing are much greater than those of failing. But because you dread failing the chance of failing appears magnified. If you finished the paper and made a reasonable attempt at everything, then, believe me, you've passed.

IF YOU THINK YOU'VE FAILED

Well, perhaps you have failed. But remember this: you haven't heard the results yet. And, believe me, huge numbers of students think that they have failed and then find that they have gained exceptionally high marks.

If you have always been rated a good student but think that you have failed, I bet you've passed easily. For good students are usually the sensitive worrying kind—and they are their own severest critics. I've met hundreds of people who have believed that they have failed exams.; but they've passed.

I remember talking to one young man who explained slowly and surely for one hour how he had failed Economics and History in his Higher School Certificate. He gave eighty-six sincere and valid reasons which made me agree that he must have failed. Imagine the surprise when the results came out and he was revealed to be in the top ten in the county!

It's natural to think that you've failed.

But it's often an optical illusion.

IF YOU THINK YOU'VE FAILED, YOU'RE LIKE MOST OF THE OTHER THOUSANDS—AND MOST OF THEM WILL HAVE PASSED!

CHAPTER FOURTEEN

TREASURE-HOUSE

STORED here are the maxims that will bring you examination glory.   Fifty points give you the key to success.

Here they are:

ON EXAMINATION SUCCESS

1.   Examination success does not always go to the man who knows most about his *subject*; it goes to the man who knows most about his *examination*.

2.   Exams. are not passed by *swotting*: they are passed by technique.

THE VALUE OF ESSAYS

1.   You can get through G.C.E. in eight subjects—by writing nothing but essays.

2.   The more advanced the exam., the more vital the essay!

RULES FOR THE GENERAL ENGLISH ESSAY

1.   Start it with an earthquake—and work up to a climax!

2.   Use the word " I "— remember, " I " starts " interest " and " individuality "!

3.   If the subject is " Guns " and you know more about " Buns "—write about " Buns " and entitle it " Guns "!

4.   Make gay essays from boring subjects.

5.   Keep words, sentences and paragraphs *short*.

6.   If you can't spell it, don't write it!

7.   If you can't punctuate it, don't write it!

8.   Your ending should echo your opening.

9.   Do the essay last!

PREPARING ADVANCED ESSAYS IN OTHER SUBJECTS

1.   Study past papers for half an hour, rather than dull books for half a year.

2. Find the minimum of work you need to do while still being able to pass the exam.

3. Prepare a minimum of essay material cleverly.

4. Use the minimum in your examination answers.

5. Write very fast, to get it all down.

6. When you don't know, bluff!

BLUFF IN YOUR ESSAYS

1. Even if you don't keep to the point, always *appear* to do so.

2. In an examination the man who shines is not the man who can write well about something he knows, but the man who can write brilliantly about something he doesn't know.

3. Quotations are helpful—especially imaginary ones!

METHODS OF STUDY

(*a*) *By Correspondence:*

1. Correspondence Courses are wonderful things—for lighthouse-keepers!

(*b*) *Teaching Yourself:*

2. He travels farthest who travels alone—if he knows the way.

(*c*) *Private Tuition:*

3. You should benefit from a teacher with the personal touch, but mind he doesn't touch you for much.

(*d*) *The Best Way:*

4. If you want to be first-class, first join a class!

NOTES

1. Three note-books: one thick main book, one soft-backed jotter: one little book always in your pocket.

2. Take note, rather than take notes.

3. Nonsense is often noteworthy.

4. Make notes from your reading—then remember the notes and forget the reading.

5. Read your note-book again and again and again and again and again and again. Then read through it again.

MELVIN POWERS SELF-IMPROVEMENT LIBRARY

ASTROLOGY
___ ASTROLOGY—HOW TO CHART YOUR HOROSCOPE Max Heindel 7.00
___ ASTROLOGY AND SEXUAL ANALYSIS Morris C. Goodman 7.00
___ ASTROLOGY AND YOU Carroll Righter 5.00
___ ASTROLOGY MADE EASY Astarte 7.00
___ ASTROLOGY, ROMANCE, YOU AND THE STARS Anthony Norvell 10.00
___ MY WORLD OF ASTROLOGY Sydney Omarr 10.00
___ THOUGHT DIAL Sydney Omarr 7.00
___ WHAT THE STARS REVEAL ABOUT THE MEN IN YOUR LIFE Thelma White 3.00

BRIDGE
___ BRIDGE BIDDING MADE EASY Edwin B. Kantar 15.00
___ BRIDGE CONVENTIONS Edwin B. Kantar 10.00
___ COMPETITIVE BIDDING IN MODERN BRIDGE Edgar Kaplan 7.00
___ DEFENSIVE BRIDGE PLAY COMPLETE Edwin B Kantar 20.00
___ GAMESMAN BRIDGE—PLAY BETTER WITH KANTAR Edwin B. Kantar 7.00
___ HOW TO IMPROVE YOUR BRIDGE Alfred Sheinwold 7.00
___ IMPROVING YOUR BIDDING SKILLS Edwin B. Kantar 10.00
___ INTRODUCTION TO DECLARER'S PLAY Edwin B. Kantar 7.00
___ INTRODUCTION TO DEFENDER'S PLAY Edwin B. Kantar 7.00
___ KANTAR FOR THE DEFENSE Edwin B. Kantar 7.00
___ KANTAR FOR THE DEFENSE VOLUME 2 Edwin B. Kantar 10.00
___ TEST YOUR BRIDGE PLAY Edwin B. Kantar 10.00
___ VOLUME 2—TEST YOUR BRIDGE PLAY Edwin B. Kantar 10.00
___ WINNING DECLARER PLAY Dorothy Hayden Truscott 10.00

BUSINESS, STUDY & REFERENCE
___ BRAINSTORMING Charles Clark 10.00
___ CONVERSATION MADE EASY Elliot Russell 5.00
___ EXAM SECRET Dennis B. Jackson 7.00
___ FIX-IT BOOK Arthur Symons 2.00
___ HOW TO DEVELOP A BETTER SPEAKING VOICE M. Hellier 5.00
___ HOW TO SAVE 50% ON GAS & CAR EXPENSES Ken Stansbie 5.00
___ HOW TO SELF-PUBLISH YOUR BOOK & MAKE IT A BEST SELLER Melvin Powers . . 20.00
___ INCREASE YOUR LEARNING POWER Geoffrey A. Dudley 5.00
___ PRACTICAL GUIDE TO BETTER CONCENTRATION Melvin Powers 5.00
___ PUBLIC SPEAKING MADE EASY Thomas Montalbo 10.00
___ 7 DAYS TO FASTER READING William S. Schaill 7.00
___ SONGWRITER'S RHYMING DICTIONARY Jane Shaw Whitfield 10.00
___ SPELLING MADE EASY Lester D. Basch & Dr. Milton Finkelstein 3.00
___ STUDENT'S GUIDE TO BETTER GRADES J.A. Rickard 3.00
___ TEST YOURSELF—FIND YOUR HIDDEN TALENT Jack Shafer 3.00
___ YOUR WILL & WHAT TO DO ABOUT IT Attorney Samuel G. King 7.00

CALLIGRAPHY
___ ADVANCED CALLIGRAPHY Katherine Jeffares 7.00
___ CALLIGRAPHY—THE ART OF BEAUTIFUL WRITING Katherine Jeffares 7.00
___ CALLIGRAPHY FOR FUN & PROFIT Anne Leptich & Jacque Evans 7.00
___ CALLIGRAPHY MADE EASY Tina Serafini 7.00

CHESS & CHECKERS
___ BEGINNER'S GUIDE TO WINNING CHESS Fred Reinfeld 10.00
___ CHESS IN TEN EASY LESSONS Larry Evans 10.00
___ CHESS MADE EASY Milton L. Hanauer 5.00
___ CHESS PROBLEMS FOR BEGINNERS Edited by Fred Reinfeld 7.00

____CHESS TACTICS FOR BEGINNERS Edited by Fred Reinfeld 7.00
____HOW TO WIN AT CHECKERS Fred Reinfeld 7.00
____1001 BRILLIANT WAYS TO CHECKMATE Fred Reinfeld 10.00
____1001 WINNING CHESS SACRIFICES & COMBINATIONS Fred Reinfeld 10.00

COOKERY & HERBS

____CULPEPER'S HERBAL REMEDIES Dr. Nicholas Culpeper 5.00
____FAST GOURMET COOKBOOK Poppy Cannon 2.50
____HEALING POWER OF HERBS May Bethel 5.00
____HEALING POWER OF NATURAL FOODS May Bethel 7.00
____HERBS FOR HEALTH—HOW TO GROW & USE THEM Louise Evans Doole 7.00
____HOME GARDEN COOKBOOK—DELICIOUS NATURAL FOOD RECIPES Ken Kraft 3.00
____MEATLESS MEAL GUIDE Tomi Ryan & James H. Ryan, M.D. 4.00
____VEGETABLE GARDENING FOR BEGINNERS Hugh Wilberg 2.00
____VEGETABLES FOR TODAY'S GARDENS R. Milton Carleton 2.00
____VEGETARIAN COOKERY Janet Walker 10.00
____VEGETARIAN COOKING MADE EASY & DELECTABLE Veronica Vezza 3.00

GAMBLING & POKER

____HOW TO WIN AT POKER Terence Reese & Anthony T. Watkins 7.00
____SCARNE ON DICE John Scarne 15.00
____WINNING AT CRAPS Dr. Lloyd T. Commins 5.00
____WINNING AT GIN Chester Wander & Cy Rice 3.00
____WINNING AT POKER—AN EXPERT'S GUIDE John Archer 10.00
____WINNING AT 21—AN EXPERT'S GUIDE John Archer 10.00
____WiNNING POKER SYSTEMS Norman Zadeh 10.00

HEALTH

____BEE POLLEN Lynda Lyngheim & Jack Scagnetti 5.00
____COPING WITH ALZHEIMER'S Rose Oliver, Ph.D. & Francis Bock, Ph.D. 10.00
____DR. LINDNER'S POINT SYSTEM FOOD PROGRAM Peter G Lindner, M.D. 2.00
____HELP YOURSELF TO BETTER SIGHT Margaret Darst Corbett 7.00
____HOW YOU CAN STOP SMOKING PERMANENTLY Ernest Caldwell 5.00
____MIND OVER PLATTER Peter G Lindner, M.D. 5.00
____NATURE'S WAY TO NUTRITION & VIBRANT HEALTH Robert J. Scrutton 3.00
____NEW CARBOHYDRATE DIET COUNTER Patti Lopez-Pereira 2.00
____REFLEXOLOGY Dr. Maybelle Segal 5.00
____REFLEXOLOGY FOR GOOD HEALTH Anna Kaye & Don C. Matchan 7.00
____30 DAYS TO BEAUTIFUL LEGS Dr. Marc Selner 3.00
____WONDER WITHIN Thomas S. Coyle, M.D. 10.00
____YOU CAN LEARN TO RELAX Dr. Samuel Gutwirth 5.00

HOBBIES

____BEACHCOMBING FOR BEGINNERS Norman Hickin 2.00
____BLACKSTONE'S MODERN CARD TRICKS Harry Blackstone 7.00
____BLACKSTONE'S SECRETS OF MAGIC Harry Blackstone 7.00
____COIN COLLECTING FOR BEGINNERS Burton Hobson & Fred Reinfeld 7.00
____ENTERTAINING WITH ESP Tony 'Doc' Shiels 2.00
____400 FASCINATING MAGIC TRICKS YOU CAN DO Howard Thurston 7.00
____HOW I TURN JUNK INTO FUN AND PROFIT Sari 3.00
____HOW TO WRITE A HIT SONG AND SELL IT Tommy Boyce 10.00
____MAGIC FOR ALL AGES Walter Gibson 7.00
____PLANTING A TREE TreePeople with Andy & Katie Lipkis 13.00
____STAMP COLLECTING FOR BEGINNERS Burton Hobson 3.00

HORSE PLAYER'S WINNING GUIDES

____BETTING HORSES TO WIN Les Conklin 7.00
____ELIMINATE THE LOSERS Bob McKnight 5.00
____HOW TO PICK WINNING HORSES Bob McKnight 5.00

___SEX WITHOUT GUILT Albert Ellis, Ph.D. 7.00
___SEXUALLY ADEQUATE MALE Frank S. Caprio, M.D. 3.00
___SEXUALLY FULFILLED MAN Dr. Rachel Copelan 5.00
___STAYING IN LOVE Dr. Norton F. Kristy 7.00

MELVIN POWERS'S MAIL ORDER LIBRARY
___HOW TO GET RICH IN MAIL ORDER Melvin Powers 20.00
___HOW TO SELF-PUBLISH YOUR BOOK Melvin Powers 20.00
___HOW TO WRITE A GOOD ADVERTISEMENT Victor O. Schwab 20.00
___MAIL ORDER MADE EASY J. Frank Brumbaugh 20.00
___MAKING MONEY WITH CLASSIFIED ADS Melvin Powers 20.00

METAPHYSICS & OCCULT
___CONCENTRATION—A GUIDE TO MENTAL MASTERY Mouni Sadhu 7.00
___EXTRA-TERRESTRIAL INTELLIGENCE—THE FIRST ENCOUNTER 6.00
___FORTUNE TELLING WITH CARDS P. Foli 10.00
___HOW TO INTERPRET DREAMS, OMENS & FORTUNE TELLING SIGNS Gettings 5.00
___HOW TO UNDERSTAND YOUR DREAMS Geoffrey A. Dudley 7.00
___MAGICIAN—HIS TRAINING AND WORK W.E. Butler 7.00
___MEDITATION Mouni Sadhu 10.00
___MODERN NUMEROLOGY Morris C. Goodman 5.00
___NUMEROLOGY—ITS FACTS AND SECRETS Ariel Yvon Taylor 5.00
___NUMEROLOGY MADE EASY W. Mykian 5.00
___PALMISTRY MADE EASY Fred Gettings 7.00
___PALMISTRY MADE PRACTICAL Elizabeth Daniels Squire 7.00
___PROPHECY IN OUR TIME Martin Ebon 2.50
___SUPERSTITION—ARE YOU SUPERSTITIOUS? Eric Maple 2.00
___TAROT OF THE BOHEMIANS Papus 10.00
___WAYS TO SELF-REALIZATION Mouni Sadhu 7.00
___WITCHCRAFT, MAGIC & OCCULTISM—A FASCINATING HISTORY W.B. Crow 10.00
___WITCHCRAFT—THE SIXTH SENSE Justine Glass 7.00

RECOVERY
___KNIGHT IN RUSTY ARMOR Robert Fisher 5.00
___KNIGHT IN RUSTY ARMOR (Hard cover edition) Robert Fisher 10.00
___KNIGHTS WITHOUT ARMOR (Hard cover edition) Aaron R. Kipnis, Ph.D. 10.00
___PRINCESS WHO BELIEVED IN FAIRY TALES Marcia Grad 10.00

SELF-HELP & INSPIRATIONAL
___CHARISMA—HOW TO GET "THAT SPECIAL MAGIC" Marcia Grad 10.00
___DAILY POWER FOR JOYFUL LIVING Dr. Donald Curtis 7.00
___DYNAMIC THINKING Melvin Powers 5.00
___GREATEST POWER IN THE UNIVERSE U.S. Andersen 10.00
___GROW RICH WHILE YOU SLEEP Ben Sweetland 10.00
___GROW RICH WITH YOUR MILLION DOLLAR MIND Brian Adams 7.00
___GROWTH THROUGH REASON Albert Ellis, Ph.D. 10.00
___GUIDE TO PERSONAL HAPPINESS Albert Ellis, Ph.D. & Irving Becker, Ed.D. 10.00
___HANDWRITING ANALYSIS MADE EASY John Marley 10.00
___HANDWRITING TELLS Nadya Olyanova 7.00
___HOW TO ATTRACT GOOD LUCK A.H.Z. Carr 10.00
___HOW TO DEVELOP A WINNING PERSONALITY Martin Panzer 10.00
___HOW TO DEVELOP AN EXCEPTIONAL MEMORY Young & Gibson 10.00
___HOW TO LIVE WITH A NEUROTIC Albert Ellis, Ph.D. 10.00
___HOW TO OVERCOME YOUR FEARS M.P. Leahy, M.D. 3.00
___HOW TO SUCCEED Brian Adams 7.00
___HUMAN PROBLEMS & HOW TO SOLVE THEM Dr. Donald Curtis 5.00
___I CAN Ben Sweetland 10.00
___I WILL Ben Sweetland 10.00
___KNIGHT IN RUSTY ARMOR Robert Fisher 5.00

___LEFT-HANDED PEOPLE Michael Barsley 5.00
___MAGIC IN YOUR MIND U.S. Andersen 10.00
___MAGIC OF THINKING SUCCESS Dr. David J. Schwartz 10.00
___MAGIC POWER OF YOUR MIND Walter M. Germain 10.00
___MENTAL POWER THROUGH SLEEP SUGGESTION Melvin Powers 3.00
___NEVER UNDERESTIMATE THE SELLING POWER OF A WOMAN Dottie Walters 7.00
___NEW GUIDE TO RATIONAL LIVING Albert Ellis, Ph.D. & R. Harper, Ph.D. 10.00
___PRINCESS WHO BELIEVED IN FAIRY TALES Marcia Grad 10.00
___PSYCHO-CYBERNETICS Maxwell Maltz, M.D. 10.00
___PSYCHOLOGY OF HANDWRITING Nadya Olyanova 7.00
___SALES CYBERNETICS Brian Adams 10.00
___SCIENCE OF MIND IN DAILY LIVING Dr. Donald Curtis 7.00
___SECRET OF SECRETS U.S. Andersen 7.00
___SECRET POWER OF THE PYRAMIDS U.S. Andersen 7.00
___SELF-THERAPY FOR THE STUTTERER Malcolm Frazer 3.00
___SUCCESS CYBERNETICS U.S. Andersen 7.00
___10 DAYS TO A GREAT NEW LIFE William E. Edwards 3.00
___THINK AND GROW RICH Napoleon Hill 10.00
___THINK LIKE A WINNER Walter Doyle Staples, Ph.D. 10.00
___THREE MAGIC WORDS U.S. Andersen 10.00
___TREASURY OF COMFORT Edited by Rabbi Sidney Greenberg 10.00
___TREASURY OF THE ART OF LIVING Sidney S. Greenberg 10.00
___WHAT YOUR HANDWRITING REVEALS Albert E. Hughes 4.00
___WONDER WITHIN Thomas F. Coyle, M.D. 10.00
___YOUR SUBCONSCIOUS POWER Charles M. Simmons 7.00

SPORTS

___BILLIARDS—POCKET • CAROM • THREE CUSHION Clive Cottingham, Jr. 10.00
___COMPLETE GUIDE TO FISHING Vlad Evanoff 2.00
___HOW TO IMPROVE YOUR RACQUETBALL Lubarsky, Kaufman & Scagnetti 5.00
___HOW TO WIN AT POCKET BILLIARDS Edward D. Knuchell 10.00
___JOY OF WALKING Jack Scagnetti 3.00
___LEARNING & TEACHING SOCCER SKILLS Eric Worthington 3.00
___RACQUETBALL FOR WOMEN Toni Hudson, Jack Scagnetti & Vince Rondone 3.00
___SECRET OF BOWLING STRIKES Dawson Taylor 5.00
___SOCCER—THE GAME & HOW TO PLAY IT Gary Rosenthal 7.00
___STARTING SOCCER Edward F Dolan, Jr. 5.00

TENNIS LOVER'S LIBRARY

___HOW TO BEAT BETTER TENNIS PLAYERS Loring Fiske 4.00
___PSYCH YOURSELF TO BETTER TENNIS Dr. Walter A. Luszki 2.00
___TENNIS FOR BEGINNERS Dr. H.A. Murray 2.00
___TENNIS MADE EASY Joel Brecheen 5.00
___WEEKEND TENNIS—HOW TO HAVE FUN & WIN AT THE SAME TIME Bill Talbert . . . 3.00

WILSHIRE PET LIBRARY

___DOG TRAINING MADE EASY & FUN John W. Kellogg 5.00
___HOW TO BRING UP YOUR PET DOG Kurt Unkelbach 2.00
___HOW TO RAISE & TRAIN YOUR PUPPY Jeff Griffen 5.00

The books listed above can be obtained from your bookstore or directly from Melvin Powers.
When ordering, please add $2.00 postage for the first book and $1.00 for each additional book.

Melvin Powers
12015 Sherman Road, No. Hollywood, California 91605